# Selling on Amazon

## A Step-by-Step Guide to Using Amazon's Seller Platform

Paul D. Gutiérrez Covey

Copyright © 2018 Paul D. Gutiérrez Covey

All rights reserved.

ISBN-13: 9781982918446

# ACKNOWLEDGEMENTS

I would like to thank my good friend, Carlos "Gerson" Salas Vindas for referring me to work at one of the greatest companies in the world, where I learned everything I know about the topic in this book. I would also like to thank Verny Mora, who taught me much of what I know about selling on Amazon, and my friend, Geancarlo Cubillo. Of course, the biggest thanks goes to my Lord, whom has guided me at all times, and has given me the wisdom to succeed in all my ways, including with this book.

# CONTENTS

Introduction ................................................................................. 1

**Getting Started** ......................................................................... 3

    Creating your account ............................................................ 3

    Adding products to your inventory ......................................... 6

    Managing Orders .................................................................. 12

    Getting Paid ......................................................................... 15

    Detail Page Information ....................................................... 16

    Fees ...................................................................................... 17

**Fulfillment by Amazon (FBA)** ................................................. 21

    Setting up FBA ..................................................................... 21

    FBA Fees ............................................................................... 26

    FBA Settings ......................................................................... 28

    Creating a Shipment Plan ..................................................... 34

    Where is My Stuff? ............................................................... 42

    Removals .............................................................................. 46

FBA Reports ........................................................................ 49

Reconciliations ................................................................. 63

Lost and Damaged Inventory ........................................ 65

**Sponsored Products** .................................................... 69

The Buy Box .................................................................... 70

Creating a Campaign ..................................................... 72

Bulk Operations ............................................................. 73

Bid+ ................................................................................... 74

Campaign Performance ................................................ 74

Reports ............................................................................ 75

**Ungating and Brand Registry** .................................... 79

Ungating .......................................................................... 79

GTIN Exemption ............................................................. 84

Brand Registry ............................................................... 87

Enhanced Brand Content ............................................. 90

Headline Search Ads .................................................... 91

Storefront ........................................................................ 93

**Performance** .............................................................................. 95

    Performance Metrics ............................................................. 96

    Feedback and Customer Reviews ........................................... 98

    A-to-Z Guarantee Claims ....................................................... 99

    Chargebacks ....................................................................... 100

    Performance Notifications ................................................... 101

    Reinstating a Suspended Account ........................................ 101

**Contacting Seller Support** ....................................................... 105

**Conclusion** ............................................................................. 109

# Introduction

Selling on Amazon has come to be a great way to get ahead. With a platform that is so well known by the customers, and so trusted as well, sellers can have such an advantage. If you are a seller and you decide to use this platform to improve your sales, you can add all of your products to your virtual inventory, send them out or have Amazon send it for you, receive reviews from the happy customers, use a relatively cheap ads service, and much more.

Although this selling platform has so many benefits, it is not always so easy to use. Some sellers can struggle with the functions, and this generates many phone calls and e-mails sent to Amazon. Although the Seller Support team is always willing to help, we all know that it is preferable if we can do things ourselves rather than have to call to find out what needs to be done, and that is the very reason for this book.

If you are interested in selling on Amazon, I urge you to continue reading this book, since here you will learn everything you need to know in order to successfully sell on this awesome platform, and you will also have the knowledge necessary to make educated decisions.

Whether you have been selling on Amazon for years, or you are only about to begin, this book is for you. Here you will learn how to begin, and you will also learn many tips that can help you to really take advantage of this platform and get the most out of it.

Please keep in mind that although this book is intended for any Amazon selling platform, it has been written using the Amazon.com platform, so although the processes are mostly the same, if you are selling in Mexico or in Europe, some parts may seem a little different.

# Getting Started

**Creating your account**

To sell on Amazon, the first thing you will need to do is to create a seller account. The website for this is services.amazon.com. In order to create your account, you need to take into account that fact that there are two different types of seller accounts; professional and individual. These are called selling plans.

With a professional selling plan, you will have to pay a monthly fee, which is the US is $39.99 (in other marketplaces you will pay a similar amount). If you choose an individual selling plan, you will not have to pay any type of monthly fee. Instead, you will pay a $0.99 fee for each sale made. That way, you will only pay when you are selling, and when you are not having such a great month, you will not pay so much.

Although both accounts are mostly the same, the individual

account does have some limitation. For example, you will not be able to use feeds (flat-files used to upload inventory in bulk), change shipping fees, etc. You will learn more about these aspects along the way, but you should know that even though they are important, they are not necessary for everyone. It all depends on the type of seller you are.

So once you have made up your mind on which selling plan you want, you can access the aforementioned website. If you are going for a professional account, then you can click the orange button that says "Start selling." If you want to be an individual seller, however, do not click that button. That will create a professional seller account.

If what you want is to create an individual seller account, you should choose a different path. Under the orange button, you will see some options that say "Benefits," "How it Works," "Pricing," etc. You should click on "Pricing." Once you have done that, you can scroll down, and you will see a chart about the two selling plans there are. Under "Individual," you will see a button that says "Sell as an Individual." Click on that, and you will begin with your account creation.

Regardless of which type of selling plan you chose, you will be taken to a screen in which you will be asked whether you want to use an existing Amazon account. If you already have a customer account, you can use the same e-mail and add the same password. Once you have done that and continued, you will be asked for your legal name, and to acknowledge that you have read the terms and conditions. Now I know that most people avoid reading all the fine print, but I do strongly recommend reading this. Once you are done, click "Next."

Your next step will be to add your address, a unique display name, a website (if you have one), a phone number, and a language. Just add the information, and click the orange button below. Depending on whether you requested a call or SMS, the button will say something different. Once you have verified your account, you can click "Next."

On the next page, you will be asked to enter your payment and deposit methods. For most Amazon websites, this information can be the same, but not for Seller Central. Here, you will need a card (preferably a credit card, since most debit cards do not work). Then, you should fill out the tax information. Once you have finished and exited the tax interview, you will have to enable Two-Step Verification, and your account will be ready to use. Please take into account that if you close your browser at any step before completing the setup, you can just log into your seller account in sellercentral.amazon.com, and you will be able to continue where you left off.

Now that your account has been created, you will see that you have a notification. At the top-left corner, there will be a flag with the number 1 on it. That means there is a notification. If the number is not there, it will be soon. Once it is there, it will tell you that you need to submit documentation just to verify your account. You will have to submit your identification and a bank statement. Once that is submitted, it will take several days, but your account will be activated completely if the documentation is accepted.

## Adding products to your inventory

If you are going to sell, you will obviously need inventory. In this section you will learn how to add the inventory to your account. However, before you do that, it is important to set the shipping settings. To set this, place the cursor over the "Settings" option on the top-right corner of your screen and click "Shipping Settings." By clicking the "Edit" button to the right of "Default Shipping," you can set the types of shipping, the amount of time you will need, and the shipping fees that your customers will pay. Please keep in mind that you receive the money they pay for shipping so that you can pay the carrier.

If you have an individual selling plan, you will be unable to change the shipping fees. If you feel that the shipping fees are not enough, then you might want to use Fulfillment by Amazon (FBA). That way, Amazon will ship your orders, so you would not have to worry about the fees. There is a whole chapter in this book regarding FBA, so you can read about it there if you are interested.

Now that you have the shipping settings taken care of, you can add the inventory. There are two options to do this: uploading products manually, or using feeds. If you chose an individual account, you will not be able to use feeds. However, I have found that for most people, they can be more tedious than helpful anyway. In the end, though, it is your decision which option is the best for you.

If you decide to upload the products manually, there are two ways to do so. First, you can look for the product on Amazon, and once you find it, you can look for the "Sell on Amazon" button and click on that. I strongly advise against that, since there are similar products that may look identical, but they are not exactly the same.

You may be wondering what the big deal is. If both products are virtually identical, what would be the problem if I use the wrong one? Well, this could actually cause many problems for you in the future. For example, if it is on Amazon, it means someone else is selling it, and if it is of inferior quality to the one you sell, you are exposing yourself to negative customer reviews on the Detail Page because other sellers are offering a product that is not as good as yours.

Another problem is that if you ever need to make any type of change, whether it be the title, the description, the image, or anything else, you will be asked for proof that the change you want is correct. The most common type of proof is a picture of the product showing the barcode. If you are not selling the same product, then the barcode will be different.

Then there is FBA. If you send the wrong product the Amazon's fulfillment centers, they may detect that the product is totally different (due to the barcode being different), so this could cause chaos in your inventory. There are more reasons, but I do not want to tire you with the many pages I could write about why this could be a bad idea. Hopefully, the reasons I already gave are enough to make up your mind.

So, if you are going to omit this option, you can read the second one ahead. In your seller account, you will see several tabs at the top. The first one is "Catalog," and the second is "Inventory." Place the cursor over the "Inventory" tab and you will see a dropdown menu. Choose the option that says "Add a Product" in order to continue.

On this page, you will see a tour in which you can click the "Get Started" button to learn more about adding products to Amazon. Considering you are reading this book, you may not need to click on it, but if you want, you can do so.

Under the tour, you will see a title that says "List a new product." Under that, you will see a search bar. Type in the UPC (the number that is underneath the barcode) to search for your product and click "Search." If your product is in Amazon's catalogue, you will see something like this:

1 to 1 of 1 Results

**The Holy Armor of God**
EAN: 9781521019399
Sales Rank:2217548
1 New & Used Offer
See all product details

⚑ Listing limitations apply

· New, Collectible, Used conditions        Sell yours

· **Refurbished condition** You are not approved to list this product and we are not accepting applications at this time.

1 to 1 of 1 Results

If this is the case, then you should click the option "Sell yours" in order to continue. In the next page, you will be able to set your SKU, price, quantity, and condition. In case you are wondering, the SKU is an internal identifier that helps the Amazon agents to differentiate it from the same product being sold by other sellers. The acronym means "Stock Keeping Unit."

If you click on "Advanced View," you will see more information that you can add, but it is not mandatory information. You can leave it blank if you want. You will also see the option to have your product fulfilled by yourself or by Amazon, which we will be covering in another chapter.

If the product does not exist in Amazon's catalogue, you will not see any results. Instead, you will see an option under the search bar that says "Create a new product listing." Click on that, and you will start creating a brand new product on Amazon.

The first thing you will need to do is categorize your product. This step is very important, so choose wisely. This will greatly impact how well customers can find your product. Then, you will be asked to enter the information about the product which could be title, brand, product ID, etc. You will see some tabs at the top where you can add even more information, like the price and quality, in the "Offer" tab.

It would be a good idea to set a handling time for your products as well. Handling time is the number of days it will take for you to ship the product. In case you are wondering what the difference is between this and the shipping settings, it is simple: The shipping settings determine how long the package will take to be delivered once it has been shipped, and the handling time only deals with how long it will take to ship it.

If you want to set a specific number of days, in the "Advanced View," in the "Offer" tab, you will see an option that says "Handling Time." Just add the number of days you will need, and that is all.

You can also add images in the "Images" tab, but you must make sure that the background is totally white. Now it does not matter how white they look to you; if they are not digitally white, then the system may reject them. If your images get rejected, there are online pages like FotoFuze that can help you turn the background totally white. Once you have finished, you can click "Save and finish."

The product that you created will be assigned a new identifier called an ASIN. This is a 10-digit code that all products on Amazon will have. Any time you receive an order or need information about your products, you will need either the ASIN or the SKU, so you should know where to find this information. Both identifiers will always be in the inventory. The SKU is to the right of the image, and the ASN is under the product name.

Now that you have finished adding your product, please do not expect it to show up in your inventory immediately. It usually takes up to 20 minutes, but depending on how the system is working at the moment, sometimes it can take more. If you created a new listing, the image will take even longer to show up, so please be patient before contacting Seller Support.

If you have to upload many products and have a professional selling plan, then you can opt for using feeds. Be aware, though, that these files can be complicated to use. If you still want to use them, then read the information ahead to learn how.

If the products you want to upload are already on Amazon's

catalogue, you will need an inventory file. This file is easy to use, since all you have to add is the identifier, an SKU, and the price. If the products are not on Amazon's catalogue, then you would need a category specific file, which are the ones that do become complicated.

In order to use a flat-file, you should go to the "Inventory" tab and click "Add Products via Upload." Then, you click on the "Download template" button and find the right file. Now that you have it, open it and fill in all the necessary information. The general rule is this: if the headers are in bold, then you need to add information. If not, then they are optional.

Once you have added all the information to the file, go to "Upload Inventory files" in the same "Add Products via Upload" page and choose the best option. Then you can upload your file. After it has finished uploading, on the same page you will see a Batch ID. You will need to wait some minutes for it to finish processing, but once that is over, you will see if there were errors or not.

If there were errors, you will see an option to download a processing report. This report will tell you all the errors there are. If you are unable to solve all the issues, contact Seller Support with the Batch ID, and they will be able to assist you. Later on in this book there is a chapter about contacting Seller Support, so if you need to do so, you can skip ahead to that chapter to find out more about this subject.

## Managing Orders

With products in your inventory, hopefully you will be receiving orders pretty soon! If you are going to fulfill your own orders, then you will want to read this section. If you are going to use FBA, then you can just skip it and go directly to the next part, since you will not be managing your orders yourself.

Whenever you receive an order, Amazon will send you an e-mail notification to let you know. Then, you will have two ways of confirming your orders; manually, or with a feed. I personally recommend doing it manually, but that is up to you. Before shipping the package, so to "Manage Orders" and print the packing slip so that you can put it in the box.

Please keep in mind that before confirming the orders, you must have already shipped them. If you have not, then put this step on hold, go and ship the order, and then come back to confirm it. If you confirm it and then ship it, this could cause some problems with your account. Amazon will know what you are doing, and since this is not the correct process, they could penalize you for it.

If you are going to confirm your orders manually, just move the cursor over the "Orders" tab and click "Manage Orders." There, you will see the date that the order was placed, the order number, the ASIN and SKU, the expected ship date, expected delivery date, the type of shipping requested, and the status. In this case, the status will be "Unshipped" if you are just going to confirm it now. Be sure to ship it and confirm it before the expected ship date, or on that same day; you will be penalized if you do not.

Once you are ready to confirm, just click the "Confirm shipment" button and add the carrier information. I strongly recommend adding a tracking number, although there are some sellers who do not add this information. After you have added all the information, click on the "Confirm shipment" button.

You can also buy the shipping if you want. What that does is that you pay Amazon for the shipping, so the label will be generated for you the print it and put it on the box, and then you take it to the carrier and just hand it over.

If you want to use a feed, it is basically the same process as with inventory. You click on the "Upload Order Related Files" option in "Orders" and download the file. You fill out the information, just like when you are confirming manually, and then upload it. That way, you can confirm more than one order at once.

If you need to cancel an order, you will see the option under the "Buy shipping" button. Do not cancel orders unless it is totally necessary. If you cancel orders often, you will be penalized. The only way that you will not be affected by cancelling is if the customer asks you to cancel it. To avoid having to cancel orders, make sure the quantity of stock you have in your inventory is completely accurate.

Now about returns, there is a whole policy to follow, but it is not too complicated. Just take into account that you must accept all returns no matter what. You are not obligated to give a refund in all circumstances, but that is another story.

So if a customer requests a refund, then you accept it. Depending on the reason why the item is being returned, you may or may not have to pay for the shipping. If the customer is just returning because he or she no longer wants it, then you do not have to pay anything. If it is because the item was received defective, then you should pay for the shipping.

Once the return request was made, you can go to the "Orders" tab and click "Manage Returns." There you will see a button for each return that says "Authorize Request." Click on that to continue with the return There you can generate a label for the customer, whether it be pre-paid or not, and then authorize it.

One very important aspect you should keep in mind is that you should not reimburse the customer until you have received the item back. Think of this scenario: You authorize a return and immediately reimburse the customer. Then, you wait for the item to return, and what you receive is a box with a rock in it. How are you going to get your money back? You already reimbursed. So wait until you receive the item, and then judge whether you can give the customer any money or not.

When reimbursing, you can charge a restocking fee, and just give a partial refund, depending on the circumstances. Be careful how you process returns and refunds, since customers always have the option of complaining about you and reporting you if they feel that you were not fair. Of course, Amazon has ways to determine whether you were right or wrong, so I am not saying you always have to give the customers what they want; instead, I just want you to be careful how you proceed on this.

## Getting Paid

You have fulfilled your first orders, but the question is, when are you going to be paid for it? There are two aspects that must be considered for this. First, the expected delivery date (EDD). Normally, money will be frozen until seven days after the EDD. This is a security measure in case there are any chargebacks or refund requests. After the seven days are over, your money will be available, and you will receive it in your next payment cycle.

The payment cycle is the second aspect to be considered. If you have an individual seller plan, your payment cycle will be every seven days. So considering that you are selling every day, you will be paid once a week. If you have a professional seller plan, your payment cycle will be two weeks. If you feel that this time range is too much to wait, you can go to the "Reports" tab and click "Payments." There you will see the report of the money you have available, and you can click the "Request transfer" button which will initiate the transfer immediately.

If you decide to request transfer, just take into account that your payment cycle will be reset. By this I mean that if you were getting paid every Wednesday, and then you requested transfer on a Monday, now you will be paid every Monday, so do not worry when the next Wednesday you are not receiving any money.

If your payment cycle has gone by and you have not received your money yet, keep in mind that depending on your bank, it can sometimes take 3 – 5 business days for the money to actually be reflected in your bank account. If after that you still have not received anything, contact Seller Support to find out what happened.

## Detail Page Information

It is important for you to know what is being reported on the Detail Page. The Detail Page is the page where the customers can see and buy your product. Make sure the title is correct, the description, the bullet points, the weight – everything! If there is any incorrect information, then this could cause returns. If any information is incorrect, just go to your inventory, and at the far right side of the product, you will see the "Edit" button. Click that, and you can edit the information.

Now, editing the information will not always guarantee that the change will be reflected automatically on the Detail Page. There is a contribution system, so if two sellers have the same product, and they both make changes, contributions are made. Amazon itself makes contributions as well. Not all contributions will go through, but that is when you will have to contact Seller Support.

On the top-right corner of your seller account, click the "Help" button. Then, at the bottom, click "Get support," and then, again at the bottom, "Can't find what you need?" Click the "Contact us" option, and you will be directed to a new page. You might see an option to write some text, which is to direct you to the help pages. I usually just write any text there and click the "Get help" button.

After that, you can close the side bar, and then you will choose "Products and inventory," then, "Product page issues," and then, "Fix a product page." Once you have done that, you will need to select the ASIN, what part you want to fix, and then provide proof. This is extremely important, because without that, no changes will be made!

It does not matter how much you try to convince Seller Support with words that your change makes total sense; if you do not have proof, they are not allowed to make the change. So what you need is either a picture of the product showing the bar code and the information that needs to be changed, the manufacturer website that shows an identifier and the information, or a catalogue that shows that information.

You can then add some comments and your contact information. Once you have submitted the request, wait for the response. As long as you submitted the correct proof, the change will be made. If Seller Support responds saying that the change was made, wait 24 to 48 hours for it to be reflected on the Detail Page.

## Fees

Whenever you sell on Amazon, you will have several fees to pay. As I had mentioned before, if you have an individual selling plan, you will pay 99 cents for each order. Other than that, you will also have to pay taxes (unless you have registered a VAT ID in the account), and also a referral fee.

A referral fee is a percentage of the sales price of your product. This percentage depends on the category; for example, some categories charge 15% while others charge only 5%. Since these percentages change every once in a while, the best thing is to look for a help page called "Selling on Amazon Fee Schedule." You can look for help pages by clicking the "Help" option on the top-right corner, next to settings.

Now referral fees can be a little complicated sometimes. Sometimes figuring out which category a certain product belongs to can be ambiguous, and you might think that you are being charged more than you should be charged. If you have any doubts regarding this, just contact Seller Support, but do not get mad if they tell you that the current category is correct.

Fortunately, most referral fees are not very high. The only one that is steep is Amazon Device Accessories, which, as I write this book, is at 45%. But other than that, most of the categories are at 15% and lower. There are some at 20%, but not many of them.

Now some people might try to trick the system and categorize their products incorrectly, choosing a category that does not charge much. I strongly advise against that, since it could cause several problems.

First, your customers might have a harder time finding your products. For example, if you are selling jewelry (for which you will normally pay 20%) and you categorize it as personal computers (for which you will pay only 6%), your products will not show up if the customer filters the search by jewelry only.

Second, Amazon takes its Detail Pages very seriously. If you are found to be taking advantage of certain loopholes, the category will be changed anyway, and your account and/or product could face some consequences. Therefore, my advice is to be honest. Yeah, you want to make money, but you are doing it thanks to a website that has one of the best reputations in the world, which improves your visibility, so pay what is due.

Now if you searched for the help page I mentioned earlier, you will see something called the "Applicable minimum referral fee." This means that if the percentage that Amazon would take is less than this amount, then you will be charged this amount anyway. For example, for office products, this fee is $1. So let's say that you are selling a desk for $5. The referral fee would be 15%, but 15% of 5 is only 0.75. When you sell this item, you will be charged $1 instead of 75 cents.

If you are using FBA, you will also be charged a fulfillment fee. I will not get into much detail about this fee here, since it will be covered in the next chapter, which deals solely with FBA.

Now so many fees may seem to be a little overwhelming, but in reality it is not so much. You should be paying taxes whether you sell through Amazon or not, so that is not anything new. The fulfillment fee is something you would have to pay for if you hire people to ship your products for you, and if that is not the case and you do not want to pay, then you always have the option of shipping them yourself. Finally, the referral fee is the only one that is something extra, but it is just fair that Amazon should receive a share of your sales since you are being allowed to use this platform to make money.

# Fulfillment by Amazon (FBA)

## Setting up FBA

FBA is a wonderful service in which you do not have to worry about fulfilling orders nor dealing with customers. Just send your products to the fulfillment centers, and Amazon will take care of the rest. You will still need to add the products to your inventory, but instead of choosing to fulfill the orders yourself, you will choose to use Fulfillment by Amazon.

You should keep in mind that this service does not mean you just have to send your stock to the fulfillment centers and wait for Amazon to do the rest. You have to set everything up in the account and create the shipment from the account, indicating which products will be sent and how many units of each.

If you already have the inventory, you can still change the fulfillment method. Next to the "Edit" button in your inventory, you will see a small button with two arrows. You can click on it and choose the "Change to Fulfilled by Amazon" option. If you want to do this to several products, then select the box at the far left side, and at the top you will see a button that says "Action on X selected," "X" being the number of items you selected. There, you will see the same option to change the fulfillment.

You will see a new screen that will say "Get Started with Fulfillment by Amazon." I know we usually do not read the small print, but I do strongly recommend that you read it in this case. You will have an option that says that you have read and accepted the agreement, so you can click on the agreement link, read it, and then confirm that you read it. Then, you can click the "Get Started with Fulfillment by Amazon" button.

After that, you will see another screen about the FBA Label Service. Normally, FBA products will use labels. You can print the labels out yourself and stick then on the products, or you can pay Amazon to do it for you. I recommend that you do it yourself, since sometimes the service is less than perfect. If you want to pay for it, then accept the service. If you want to put the labels on yourself, then decline.

---

**FBA Label Service**

An item label must be affixed to each Unit for which you do not use the Stickerless, Commingled Inventory option. For qualifying Units, Fulfilment by Amazon can apply the labels on your behalf. By choosing the FBA Label Service option, you agree to allow Amazon to label your Units in accordance with the Amazon Services Business Solutions Agreement, FBA Label Service Pricing, and the below terms.

**Minimum Qualifications**

- **Condition:** Any (New, Used, Collectible, Refurbished)
- **Product Type:** Any (Media and Non-media) not prohibited by our product restrictions
- **ASIN:** Each Unit must have a scannable barcode (ISBN, UPC, EAN or JAN). If there is no scannable barcode, you will need to apply item labels yourself.

**If you sign up for FBA Label Service:**

- We will, in our sole discretion, determine which of your units qualify for the FBA Label Service. We reserve the right to disqualify Units that meet the above minimum qualifications.
- We will label your qualifying Units in the fulfillment center using the product information you provide for such Units.
- You will be charged the labeling fees specified in FBA Label Service Pricing.
- You can opt out on a per-shipment basis to label Units yourself.
- Your qualifying Units may be split into multiple additional shipments.

**If you decline this service:**

You will be responsible for applying item labels yourself. You can still use Stickerless, Commingled Inventory for Units that qualify for that option.

You can modify your Label Service preferences at any time by going to Settings > Fulfillment by Amazon.

○ Accept Label Service
○ Decline Label Service

Now you will see a page in which you will select either the Manufacturer Barcode or Amazon Barcode. Manufacturer Barcode is the UPC barcode that is already on your product. If you choose that option, it will mean that your products will be commingled. This has its advantages, but it can also be dangerous.

If two sellers are sending the same product to the fulfillment center and they are both commingled, then they are put into the same bin. When there is a sale, the agent who is packing the product will just go to the bin and take out the first one that is found. It could be yours, or it could be from another seller. In normal circumstances, this will not be a problem. But what if the other seller sent a defective item? Then you will be affected for something that is another seller's fault.

If you know for a fact that you are the only seller of the product, then you can opt for commingled inventory. However, not all items can be commingled, so sometimes, you will see that a product will need an Amazon Barcode. For example, if your product has an expiration date, then it cannot be commingled.

If you choose to use an Amazon Barcode, then your products will get something called "FNSKU" (Fulfillment Network SKU). This is a ten-digit code that will usually start with "X00." Each product that you send to the fulfillment center should have the FNSKU label which will have the code and a barcode. That way, when someone purchases the item, you can be sure that only your item will be sent.

Once you have made up your mind about which barcode you want, you will see a page in which you can choose to convert only, or to convert and send inventory. If you want to send it immediately, choose the "Convert & Send Inventory" button. If you are not going to send them immediately, then choose the "Convert Only" button.

Depending on what you chose on the previous screen, you may also see the option to choose the barcode type. Choose well, and click whichever button suits your situation the best.

The next page you will see will be for dangerous goods information. It does not matter what type of product you sell – you will always have to fill this information out. Click the "Add dangerous goods information" option and answer the questions honestly. After that, click "Submit," and then "Save & Continue."

Depending on what you answered, your product might go to Hazmat Review. You may not find out immediately, but when you try to create a shipment, the system will not allow you to send this item, and it will tell you the reason. If this happens, do not panic. Just contact Seller Support and ask how to proceed. The process can be different depending on the circumstances, so they will let you know what the best course of action is.

Finally, depending on whether you chose to convert only or to convert and send inventory, you will either be directed to the "Amazon-Fulfilled Inventory" page or the shipment creation page. We will deal with shipment creation later on, so for now I will focus on the inventory. This page is very similar to the normal inventory page. You will see your products, the price, quantities, and others. In the next paragraphs, you will learn about what some of the unique parts mean.

On this page, you will see "Inbound," "Fulfillable," "Unfulfillable," and "Reserved." "Inbound" is the number of units you have sent. As you will see later on, before actually shipping the items to the fulfillment center, you will have to create the shipment on your seller account. While doing so, you will indicate how many units of each product you want to send, so that number will be reflected here. If there are inbound units, that means that they are not in your inventory yet, so they will not be selling.

"Fulfillable" and "Unfulfillable" units are pretty straightforward. Either they are in good condition to send to the customers, or they are not. If there are any damaged units, they will show up as "Unfulfillable." There can be several reasons for your units to be in this status, but to see the exact reason, you should go to your inventory (Not the FBA Inventory). You will see more about that later on as well.

If units are "Reserved," it means that they are temporarily unable to be sold. Again, there are several reasons for this, and that can be seen in your inventory. Just like for "Unfulfillable" units, you will see more about this later on.

You will also see a "Fee Preview" and the "Unit Volume." The "Fee Preview" will tell you exactly how much Amazon is going to take from the sale, and the "Unit Volume" tells you how much room each unit takes up. This is important because every month you will have to pay a storage fee. This fee changes from time to time, but basically it is a fee you will have to pay that is calculated per cubic foot.

## FBA Fees

The fees that you will pay for FBA are different from the ones mentioned in the first chapter. The referral fee is a percentage, but FBA fees are fixed amounts. There are several different types of fees that you will have to pay for using FBA. They are the fulfillment fees, storage fees, and long-term storage fees.

Fulfillment fees can change at any moment, and usually they do, so I will not be giving any specifics. You can contact Seller Support to request that they give you a chart that will show this information. What you need to keep in mind is that what you will pay depends entirely on the dimensions and weight of your products. The bigger they are, the more you will have to pay for Amazon to ship them out.

When it comes to fulfillment fees, you are just paying for Amazon to pick, pack, and ship your items. If you did not use FBA, you would probably have to pay someone to do that work for you, so this way, Amazon pays someone to do it, and you pay Amazon for this service.

Storage fees are a different matter; you will have to pay this fee whether you sell or not. Because of this, it is very important that you think very carefully about how much stock you are going to send to the fulfillment center. If you are the kind of seller that sells a lot, then it may not make much of a difference. But if you do not sell much, then it might be a good idea to avoid sending too much of your stock.

Again, since the amount changes, I will not specify how much you will have to pay, but that is easy to find. Just search the help pages by using the keywords "Storage fees," and you will find it in no time. What you should keep in mind, though, is that there are two separate amounts per year. For example, as I write this, from January to September, you will pay $0.69 per cubic foot for standard-size stock, and from October to December you will pay $2.40 per cubic feet for standard-size.

I know that the difference seems substantial, but that is because from October to December a lot of people are buying from Amazon for Christmas, so it is very possible that your sales will increase at this time of year anyway. You may have noticed, also, that in the previous paragraph I mentioned standard-size. That is because there is a difference between what you will pay for standard-size and oversize.

The long term storage fee is charged twice a year; once in February, and a second time in August. If you have any products that have been in the fulfillment center for any number of days between 181 and 365, then you will have to pay a fee. Again, this could change, but as I write this, you will pay $11.25 per cubic foot if the number of days is between 181 and 365. If they have been stored for more time, then you will pay $22.50.

This last fee may seem to be steep, but you can avoid paying so much. One way is to pay attention to how much time your stock has been in the fulfillment center. That can be pretty tricky, so instead of that, you can also check the FBA settings, which will be covered in the next section.

## FBA Settings

Make sure you check your FBA settings before you start selling. If you do not set these up to your likings, you may regret it later on. Here you will find Optional Services, Inbound Settings, Repackaging Settings, Automated Unfulfillable Removal Settings, Automated Long-Term Storage Removals Settings, FBA Product Barcode Preference, Subscription Settings, Multi-Channel Fulfillment Settings, Partnered Carrier Programs, Product Support, Export Settings, and Giveaways Settings. In this section I will walk you through each of them so you can set your FBA settings up perfectly according to your specifications.

Finding these settings is very easy. On the top-right corner of your seller account, you will see the settings option. Do not click it; just hover the cursor over it, and select "Fulfillment by Amazon."

First we have the Optional Services. We already covered some of these services before when we were talking about setting up FBA, but here is where you can change them. The services you will find here are the label service, in which you can pay Amazon to put the FNSKU labels on for you, the default settings of who will prepare your stock (in other words, adding extra packaging, for example), and the default of who will label the products that you will send.

Next you will see the Inbound Settings. There, the first setting you will see is Inventory Placement Option. Normally, when you are creating a shipment, the system may direct you to send the units in several different shipments to different fulfillment centers. This is done to ensure that your customers will be able to have more availability to receive your products and that they can receive them faster.

Of course, this can be tedious and cost more money, so Amazon implemented this service to avoid that kind of trouble. If you enable it, you will only have to send to one fulfillment center, and then from their they will be distributed to the others. Some categories are not eligible for the Inventory Placement Service, but most of them are.

What you should take into account, when deciding whether to use this service or not is the fact that it will take longer for your stock to become available. Normally, when you send the units, they become available as soon as they are received and processed. But in this case, once they are processed, they will be sent to another fulfillment center, and so it will take longer before the customers can purchase them.

Another aspect to keep in mind is that you will have to pay a per-unit service fee for this service. This may not matter so much, since you will have to pay extra for the shipping if you have to ship to many different fulfillment centers, but this is something you should take into consideration before making a decision.

The second option you will see in Inbound Settings is to Show Restricted Items Warning. Although many items can be sold on Amazon, not all of them can be sold with FBA. For example, certain types of hazardous materials must be fulfilled by you instead of by Amazon.

This option is very straightforward; either you want to see the warning or you do not. In my opinion, this is a no-brainer. The best course of action is to enable it so that you do not try to send something that cannot be sold, since sending it will cost you money, just to find out that you will have to pay to have it returned to you instead of selling it.

The following option is similar to the first, but this time it is about products that, although they can be sold, require a special approval. If you need to obtain approval for a certain category, I will cover this subject later on, but for now you just know that enabling this option will allow you to receive warnings whenever you list an item that requires approval.

The final option you will see on this section of the settings is the 2D Barcodes for Box Content Information. Normally, when you send a box to the fulfillment center, they will open the box and scan each item one by one in order to process them. If you add this barcode on the box, it will have all the information of what exactly is in the box, so in this way, they will only have to scan this barcode, and all the contents of the box will be processed at once.

This option can help speed up the process of receiving your stock and making it available; however, you must make sure that everything you indicated that would be in that box really is there. If not, the contents will be processed, but then when they find that not everything is there, it will be unprocessed.

This may not seem like a big deal, but I will give you an example so that you can understand better. Maybe it still will not be a big deal, but for some it could be.

Imagine that you indicated in shipping plan that you would

send ten books, but you only added nine. When the barcode on the box is scanned, you will see in your inventory that there are ten units available. However, when they open the box to put the units in the bin, they will find that only nine are there, so when you look at the inventory again, you will see only nine units.

The third set of settings you will see are the Repackaging Settings. Sometimes customers will return items that are not sellable anymore because of the packaging. If you choose to enable this setting, Amazon will repackage them and sell them as new once again. If you like this feature, you can enable it.

You will see a list of categories that this setting is eligible for. If your products are in any other category, then they will not be repackaged. You can select or deselect any of the categories in the list, in case there are certain types of products that you prefer not to use this service for.

Now there may come times when Amazon will update the list of categories and add new ones. If you want them to automatically be enrolled in this service, then you can select the auto-enroll option, and then select whether you would like to receive an e-mail every time a category is added.

Next is Automated Unfufillable Removal Settings. There will be times in which there will be unsellable inventory in the fulfillment center. One reason could be because a customer damaged it and then returned it. Another reason could be because the customer returned it saying that it was defective. There are more reasons why it could be unsellable, but this feature will help to remove the products automatically.

Removal means that Amazon will send you some of your units back, so if you have this setting enabled, then anytime there is damaged inventory, it will be shipped back to you automatically without you having to request it.

The next setting is very similar to the previous one. It is called Automated Long-Term Storage Removals Settings. In the previous section, I mentioned that you would have to pay a long-term storage fee, but that you could avoid it either by keeping an eye on how long your inventory was there, or you could check the FBA settings. This section of the settings is where you can take care of that so as to not have to pay so much.

If you enable this setting, your stock will be removed before you would have to pay for the long-term storage fee, thus never having to pay it at all. If you do not mind paying this fee, then you can disable it. Some find it easier to just pay than to have to receive it and then ship it back to the fulfillment center again. The decision is yours to choose which is the best course of action!

The following setting is for FBA Product Barcode Preference. We already covered this when we were getting started with FBA, but in case you changed your mind, you can change your preference here. Just a reminder, this is to choose whether you want to use the FNSKU label or to just leave the manufacturer barcode without any extra labels.

Under that settings option, you will find Subscription Settings. Amazon has a feature for the customers called "Subscribe & Save" in which they can receive discounts for the products they buy. Enrolling your products could help your chances of selling.

Depending on several factors, you may or may not be eligible for this program. In order to be eligible, you should be selling with FBA for at least 3 months, you should have an overall feedback rating of 4.7, and you should be in good standing, meaning that your seller metrics should be good. I will cover metrics in another chapter, so you can learn more there.

Multi-Channel Fulfillment Settings are next up. Multi-Channel Fulfillment will be covered later on, but for now what you need to know is that this is a type of fulfillment that can be done for orders that are not from Amazon. You can choose to have your name on the packing slip that will be sent to the customer, and you can set an extra text.

After that you will see the Partnered Carrier Programs, but there is nothing that can be done here. I am not even sure why it is showing in these settings since there is nothing you can really set. It is just there to let you know that you can use the partnered carrier for LTL shipments. Depending on the marketplace you are selling on, you may not see this option enabled here, like for example in the European marketplaces.

You will then see Product Support. Basically, this means whether or not you will receive messages from the customers. Since Amazon will be providing customer service for your orders, you might want to keep this option disabled. However, if you are selling products that might require your technical support, Amazon will not provide that kind of support, so you will need to enable this option.

The second to last one you will see is Export Settings. You

can choose whether or not you will allow FBA to ship to other countries. Of course, the fact that your products can be exported will give you more chances of selling, but you decide whether you really want that or not.

Finally, you will see the Giveaways Settings. Enabling this means that customers can host giveaways of your products. This does not mean that you will be giving anything for free; instead, the person hosting the giveaway will pay for your product and give it to someone else for free. Usually this is done for contests and raffles. Keep in mind that if you have an individual selling plan, you will not be able to enable Giveaways.

## Creating a Shipment Plan

You are now ready to ship your stock to the fulfillment center in order to start selling. You have already converted your stock, learned about the fees, configured your FBA settings, so now you just have to send your products.

This is not a matter of just packing the items into a box and sending them; you have to create the shipping plan first, and then send it. This is not complicated at all. In this sections, you will see each of the steps and learn exactly what needs to be done.

First, you need to go to your Amazon-Fulfilled Inventory. In order to reach that page, hover the cursor over the "Inventory" tab and click "Manage FBA Inventory." Once you are there, you will see all the products that you have converted to FBA. To the left, you will see that each of them have a little checkbox. Click these checkboxes for each product you want to ship, and above you will see a message that says "Apply to X Selected Item(s)" (X being the number of items selected). Next to that, you will see a drop-down menu. Click on it, select the option "Send/replenish inventory," and click "Go."

If this is your first plan, you will need to set an address. Under where it says "Ship from," you can add your address. Then, you will need to choose between "individual products" and "case-packed products."

Individual products means that you have different types of products in one box. So for example, if you are sending different types of phones, obviously you can send many in one box, since they are small. If you can fit all of them in the same box, you would choose individual.

Case-packed products means that every box has only one type of item. So using the same example of the phones, if you are going to send three different types, and you are sending enough that you need three boxes, then you would choose case-packed so that you can pack one type of phone per box, so each box will only have one type of phone each. Once you have selected the packing type, click "Continue to shipping plan."

The next step in the plan is to set the quantities. You will see three tabs here; "All products," "Information required," and "Removal required." "All products" will show each of the products that you have selected for the plan. You will see boxes to the right in which you will type in the number of units you will ship. You may also see some more boxes in which you will have to add the measurements of the box(es) and the weight of the units. If so, add the information and click "Save." Make sure that the weight that you add is completely accurate. Do not guess, because this could cause some problems later on.

In the "Information required" tab, you will see any products that require for you to add information to them. For example, if you needed to add weight and dimensions to any products, they would show up in this tab. If you have many items in your plan, this tab is useful to filter only the items that require you to add something so that you can add everything easily.

In the "Removal required" tab, you will see any products that cannot be shipped to the fulfillment center. The most common type of products that you might see here are hazmat types. If there is anything here, contact Seller Support to find out why. If you need to remove it, just go back to the "All products" tab, and to the left you will see an option to remove them.

When you have finished with this section, click the

"Continue" button, and you will be taken to the "Prepare Products" page. If any of your products need any special preparation, you can choose to do it yourself or to pay Amazon to do it. You will have to choose the category, and then, if it is a type of product that requires preparation, you will see a drop-down menu to the right in which you can choose who will prepare them.

Not all products will need this special preparation. The ones that do are products that that have any of the following characteristics:

- Baby products
- Sharp
- Fragile
- Clothing on hangers
- Cloths or fabrics
- Very small
- Adult
- Liquids that are not in glass containers
- Powder, pellets, and granular
- Perforated packaging.

The type of preparation that you may need could be poly bagging, bubble wrap, opaque bagging, or taping. While you are in this section of the FBA Inbound Workflow (which is what the shipment preparation page is called), you will see a link on the top-right corner that says "View prep help." There you will see all the types of products that need preparation, and by clicking on them, you will see what type.

Right next to the "View prep help" option, you will see an

option that says "Seller University Video." I recommend clicking on that, since it will show you a video on how you can prepare your products correctly. Once you have chosen who will prepare them, click the "Continue" button.

Now we have reached the labeling section. If your products do not require the FNSKU label, then there is nothing to really do here, so you can just continue. If your products do require labels, then here you will choose whether you will put them on or if Amazon will.

Personally, I recommend that you put them on yourself for several reasons. First, if you send them all ready with the labels on, they will be processed much faster and will be ready to sell in no time, whereas if Amazon has to do it, processing will take longer because of this.

On the other hand, barcodes can have some issues sometimes that can cause confusion in the fulfillment centers, and it could cause some problems; not to mention the fact that even when there are no confusing issues, they do not always get it right. In order to avoid problems, just put them on yourself.

If you do decide that Amazon will label your products, just choose "Amazon" in the drop-down menu and click "Continue." If you do it yourself, then choose "Merchant," and then below that, you will see a button that says "Print labels for this page." Choose the paper type and then click that button in order to generate a PDF file with the barcodes for the products in your shipment.

In my personal seller account, I created a shipment with a Spanish book called "*Las Aventuras de Sherlock Holmes.*" In the following image, you will see the FNSKU label, which shows a barcode, the FNSKU code, the name of the product, and the condition it is in:

Print the labels (preferable on sticker paper), and put them on your products over the manufacturer barcode. This is very important, because if the FNSKU label and the manufacturer barcode are showing at the same time, this will cause confusion; only one should be showing. A good practice is to put transparent tape over the barcode, then add the label over the tape, and then add more transparent tape over the label. That way the buyer can remove the label easily if needed.

Once you have finished with this page, you can click the "Continue" button once again. The next page you will see is "Review Shipments." Here you will see how many shipments will be created, and to which fulfillment centers. You can name each shipment, which could help if you keep records of everything and want to find it easily. If everything is correct, just click the "Approve shipments" button to continue.

It is possible that now you will see multiple shipments on the next page. If so, you will have to take the next steps one by one on each of them. If that is the case, just click on the "Work on shipment" button for one of the shipments, and you will be taken to the "Prepare Shipment" page.

On this page, you will have to choose your carrier. If you are shipping pallets, then you will have to choose less than truckload (LTL). If your shipment is less than 150 lb, then you will not use pallets, and you should choose small parcel delivery (SPD).

After choosing the shipping method, you will be able to choose between the Amazon-Partnered Carrier or any other one. I strongly recommend the partnered carrier for several reasons. If any items are damaged on the way, Amazon will investigate, and they will pay for the units. Of course, if you damaged them before you shipped them, Amazon will know, and you will not receive a dime, so do not try to trick the system, because it will not work.

Another reason is because UPS and FedEx work almost perfectly with Amazon's system, and any claim you may have to make will be so much easier. With any other carrier, they will have to make an appointment with Amazon, and it can be very complicated for them. They may ask you to do it, but that is not your job; the carrier has to do it, because only they have all the information needed to do so.

If you do choose the Amazon-Partnered Carrier, you will pay directly to Amazon, and you will receive a discount for it. In reality, it is a win-win situation; you pay less and receive better service, so I believe that it is the best option to choose.

After choosing the carrier, you will have to set the packaging information. You can use a web form, in which you just add the information on the same page, upload a file, or skip this information.

If you choose the use the web form, you just have to fill in the boxes with the dimensions and weight. I cannot stress enough how important it is that the information be totally accurate. Incorrect weight can automatically disqualify you from getting a refund for lost items. The same goes for when you report the weight to the carrier you use.

If you choose to upload a file, you will choose the file format, add the number of boxes, and then click on the "Generate pack list template" button. Fill out the form, and then click the "Upload now" button so that you can upload the file.

Choosing to skip the information will cause an additional fee to be applied. At this moment, the fee is $0.10 per unit, although in the future it might be different. You will not have to add any information; instead, Amazon will calculate it all the first time you ship it, and then it will populate automatically the next time you send the same ASINs.

Finally, you will be asked to print the labels for the boxes. Choose your paper type, and then click on the "Print box labels" button to generate a PDF with the labels that you will need to stick on the boxes. If you are sending pallets, you will need to put labels on all four sides.

If you are using the Amazon-Partnered Carrier, you will also see a button to accept the charges. If you chose a different carrier, you will have to pay them directly, since Amazon will have no association with them. Regardless of which option you have chosen, you will see a button that says "Complete shipment." Click on that, and then you can ship.

If you did not choose the partnered carrier, you will still have one final step after you have shipped your products. On the final page of the shipment, you will see the "Summary." Add the tracking information and then click the "Mark as shipped" button that is above where you just entered that information, and now just wait for it to be delivered.

Keep in mind that in any part of the shipment creation, if you need to stop and shut down your computer, you can do so, and the next time you log in, you can hover the cursor over "Inventory" and click the "Manage FBA Shipments" option where you will see an option to continue with your shipment. You can also delete your shipment at any time. At the bottom of the page for any shipment, you will see a "Delete" button.

## Where is My Stuff?

There may come times in which you ship items to the fulfillment centers, and not everything arrives. If this occurs, do not panic; as long as you did everything right, you will be compensated for the missing items. It is a simple process, but it could take some days.

The important thing to keep in mind is that if you see that your shipment was delivered, but not everything has been processed, just wait. The items go to your inventory in real time, so there is a good chance that they just have not been processed yet, and that they did not finish.

Now if the shipment was delivered on a Monday, and by

Friday there are still some items missing, then it probably means that they are missing. Do not contact Seller Support yet, though, because they will not be able to help just yet. Before they can start investigating, fourteen days must have gone by after the delivery date.

I know that two weeks may seem like a long wait, but there is a reason for this. In the past, it used to be just three days. However, they noticed that in many cases, they would reimburse the seller, but then in the two week period, the missing items were found and processed, so the refund was taken back. This caused a lot of confusion since, obviously, if you see that you are being charged, you are going to want to know why.

If you have waited the 14-day period and there are still items missing, then it is time to open up an investigation. To do this, do not open up a normal case like you would to contact for any other issue; instead, you should go to the shipment summary. There, you will see a tab that says "Conciliation." Click on that, and if your shipment is eligible for investigation, it will give you the option to request said investigation.

In some cases, you will have extra items as well. Always request investigation for overages, no matter what. This will delay the process for a couple days, but trust me, you will receive a more accurate solution for the missing items if there are any.

Sometimes, the extra items (also called overages) are virtual. This means that they were just a counting error, and they never actually existed. If this is the case, you will receive a response telling you this, and they will send you a link to the FBA reports (which will be covered more in detail in a future section). There is one report called "Inventory Adjustments" where you will see misplaced items. This does not mean that they lost your stock, but that they corrected the quantity of the overages by marking them as misplaced in this report.

In other cases, the overages could have been misprocessed, and they are actually the missing items (also called shortages), so they would only have to re-process them as the correct items. There are other cases in which the mistake was not even Amazon's. Sometimes it could be that you sent an item that had one barcode as if it were another, so Amazon did process it correctly, but maybe you did not add it correctly to your inventory. If that is the case, they will send you pictures to confirm it.

When requesting investigation, always add tracking ID and/or Proof of Delivery (POD). The POD must be either signed or stamped by an Amazon representative. If you used the partnered carrier, then you do not need to provide this, because it is already in the system. If not, you should request the POD from the carrier so you can send it. Keep in mind that all LTL shipments will require the stamped POD.

If the value of the missing items is more than $1000, you will also be required to provide an invoice of the products that you shipped. This cannot be a commercial invoice, and since it is meant to prove that you actually did buy the units and shipped them, the date must be earlier than the shipping date.

This invoice will not affect the refund value if reimbursement is necessary; it is only to prove that you did in fact purchase them.

In some cases, if the value is very high and you have sent multiple shipments with the same items, they may ask your for additional invoices.

Once you have submitted the request with the documentation, the investigation begins. They may contact you to provide additional documentation; do not get mad, they will not be able to investigate if what you send does not meet all the requirements.

If they have everything they need, they will do their best to find the shortages. If they do not, there are several scenarios that could happen before they reimburse. If there are true overages, they could be used to substitute the shortages. For example, if you sent two different types of laptops, but there was one missing from one type and an overage of the other type, they will say that you sent one instead of the other, and the missing laptop will not be reimbursed.

Substitutions are the reason why you need to make sure that what you indicated in the shipment details in your account is really what you are shipping, and that you are not shipping anything more nor less, and it is also one of the biggest reasons why you should request investigation for the overages. Maybe that extra laptop was really the missing one, and they just processed it incorrectly.

Sometimes they will find your items in another shipment. Do not confuse this for a substitution. There are times in which the fulfillment center agents will find units and will not know where they belong, so they will assign them to just any shipment, even if it was delivered a month ago. If this happens, trust them; they can get in trouble if they lie to you about that, and they have no reason to do so anyway. Just keep a record of your shipments. If one shipment had no errors, but now a month later there are 5 overages, and your current shipment has 5 shortages of the same item, then it means that they are telling the truth.

If there are still missing items after trying to substitute, they will check the weight. If you reported one weight to the carrier, but Amazon was expecting a different weight, you might not receive your money back. There is a 20% margin of error, so it does not mean that you will lose out for half of a pound, but you do need to report accurately.

Here is how it works; all ASINs have a weight reported in the system. Make sure that the weight of each of your ASINs is reported correctly, or else this will cause major discrepancies. So if you are shipping 10 items that are reported to be two pounds each, then Amazon is expecting twenty pounds. But if they actually weight half of a pound each, then you may be reporting only five pounds, and so there will be a weight discrepancy.

If you do not have any true overages and the weight was reported correctly, then you will most likely get your money back, or they will find your items. Amazon does not want you to lose out, so just do everything honestly and correctly, and you will be compensated.

## Removals

There may come times in which you will have to remove items from the fulfillment center. This could be because they are damaged, you no longer want to sell them, or for any other reason. When creating a removal order, you could choose to actually remove the items, which means that Amazon will ship them back to you, or to dispose of them, which means that your items will be destroyed.

If you have set up the automatic removals in the FBA settings, then you may not have to go through this very often, since any damaged or aged products will be shipped back to you automatically. If you do not have that setting activated, however, then you may need to go through this process pretty often to remove your inventory.

In order to remove your inventory, head over to the Amazon-Fulfilled Inventory, and select the units you would like to remove. Then click the drop-down menu with the default of "Send/replenish inventory," select "Create Removal Order," and then click "Go."

If this is your first removal order, you will be asked to add an address, although that is only if you are going to actually remove them instead of disposing of them. You will only be able to add an address of the country of the platform from which you are removing. If you are removing from the US platform, but you live in another country, you will have to upload a flat-file to remove your products.

On the same page in which you would add your address, at the top-right corner you will find a button that says "Upload Flat File." Click that button if you wish to remove to another country. There you will see the option to download the template. Download it, add all the necessary information, and save it as a tab-delimited file. Then upload it to the same page in which you downloaded the template.

Once you have uploaded it, you will see a batch ID and the status. If you filled it out correctly, it will process with no problem. If not, you will see some errors, and you will have the option to download a report in which you can see what errors were found so that you can correct them.

If you are not going to upload a flat-file, just enter your address, and then at the bottom of the page, enter the number of fulfillable units and the number of unfulfillable units you would like to remove, and then click "Continue." Before clicking this button, you can add an order ID if you want, but this is option. If you do not, an ID will be assigned to it automatically. This is in case you want to keep a specific record.

The next page you will see will be a summary of the removal

order that you are placing. Look at all the details to make sure everything is correct, and if it is you can go ahead and click the "Place Order" button. Now you will be able to find your order along with the normal customer orders.

## FBA Reports

It is crucial that you understand how to use the FBA reports so that you can know what is happening with your inventory. In order to access this feature, hover your cursor over the "Reports" tab and click "Fulfillment." Here you will find many different types of reports that can help you find out how your FBA inventory is doing. The first type of reports you will find are the inventory reports.

**Restock Inventory Report:**

This report, as the name suggests, will let you know which products should be restocked. This is done by taking into account how many units you have in stock and how many sales you have made. Just click the "Request Download" button, and a report will be generated with this information for you to look at.

Once the report has been generated, you can open it up and see which products are recommended for restocking. The default program to open it is Notepad, but I recommend right-clicking to choose to open it as an Excel document.

Now this is only a recommendation; you are not obligated to actually restock them, and it is based on algorithms, so ultimately, you decide whether you want to or not. That is why it is a good idea to look at the report to see why the products are being recommended, and that way, you can make an educated decision.

**Stranded Inventory:**

Stranded inventory means any units that are in the fulfillment center, but are not currently being sold. This could happen because of a blocked ASIN, Hazmat issues, or many other reasons, but the important thing is to take a look at which products are stranded so you can find a solution.

The report can be downloaded the same way that the previous one was, and there you will see important information that can help you to determine why your products are stranded. Once you have determined the reason, you can try to solve it, or you can contact Seller Support so that they can give you more information.

**Reserved Inventory:**

This report is very simple. Basically, it tells you how many units are in reserved status, and why. The reason can be pretty vague, sometimes, so for more information, you may have to contact Seller Support, but the main reasons are because of customer orders, transshipments from one fulfillment center to another, and processing.

FC Processing is the one reason that can be vague, since it could be a number of reasons. There could be some kind of investigation on these units, or the isle where they are stored could be having some maintenance. Usually this will not last too long, though.

**Subscribe & Save Forecasting:**

If you are enrolled in the "Subscribe & Save" program, this report will help you find all the information about how your products might be doing in the future. When you request a report here, you will need to specify a certain date.

Once you have downloaded the report, you will see a forecast of this program. You can see expected discounts to be applied, active subscriptions, number of items scheduled for this program for specific weeks, etc. All in all, this report will help you to plan the enrollment of this service to improve your sales.

**Inventory Reconciliation:**

At times, you may want to know all the movements of your inventory. For example, what has been shipped to the fulfillment center, what has been sold, how many units were returned, etc. This report will tell you exactly that. It is designed to help you find out what is happening with your stock. This can help you plan your shipments better.

Although this tool can be useful to find out which items are selling the most, it is not always the most accurate if you want to know why you think you should have ten units when you only have nine. For that, you may want to perform a manual reconciliation, which you will see later on.

**Small & Light Inventory:**

Small & Light Inventory is a program that allows you to sell cheap products without a minimum order requirement. Normally, if a product is less than $15, it will be add-on, and it will require that the customer order enough products so that the total will be more than the $15.

If you are interested in this program, click the "Learn more" option at the top of this reports page, and then on the help page you will see, click the "FBA Small and Light" link. This will direct you to a help page that will help you to enroll your products into the program.

Now back to the report itself, here you will see all the products that are enrolled, your current price, and how many units are in the fulfillment center. The report itself does not have much information on it that other reports do not have, but it is good to track how many units are in stock for these products.

**Amazon Fulfilled Inventory:**

At this point, you will see an option that says "Show more" in the "Inventory" section of the reports. Click that, you will see more reports that deal specifically with your FBA inventory.

This report shows you most of the information that you will see in your inventory page, except that you can download it to view in an Excel spreadsheet. This could be useful if you are keeping records of your inventory, but if that is not the case, then you will not need to access this report. Instead, you can view the normal inventory page, or the FBA inventory, which shows all the same information and more.

**Daily Inventory History:**

This report will tell you where and how your stock has been for any time-frame. Every day, the fulfillment center agents will check you inventory and report the location, quantity, and status of it. That way, if you need to know that status of your products for the last week, you can look in this report to find this information.

An example of how this could be useful is this; if you have some units that are damaged and you want to know exactly when they were damaged, you can go to this report and find the first day that it was reported as such. You can also see the updated quantities for each day if you want.

**Monthly Inventory History:**

This report is very similar to the previous one, except that instead of being reported daily, it is done once a month. That way, you can track the status of your products by the day or by the month depending on what you need to find out.

**Received Inventory:**

Here is where you will see all the stock that has been received at the fulfillment centers. You will see the date, the FNSKU, the SKU, product name, quantity, shipment ID, and the fulfillment center where it was received (regardless of where it is at now).

This report can be useful if you are trying to find out how much you have sent versus how much has been received (in case there are times in which not everything arrives), or to find out how much you have sent versus how much you have now.

**Inventory Event Detail:**

This report will show you a history, almost like the daily and monthly history reports, except that you will not see so much information. Instead, you will only see reports of when there was been any type of event. This could include all types of adjustments, sales, etc.

**Inventory Adjustments:**

This is a very important report to keep an eye on. Any important type of adjustment will go here. If any units were lost, you will find out here. Then, you will find out if they were found or not. You can also find when any unit is damaged in the warehouse.

When there are virtual overages in a shipment, they will show up here as misplaced, and when there are shortages that are later found, you can find them here, showing up as found.

**Inventory Health:**

Here, you will find an overview of your stock. You can see here how old your inventory is, how many sales have been made, how many units are sellable or unsellable, etc. This can be very useful to help you plan your next shipments to the fulfillment centers and avoid sending too much.

By looking at this information, you will know all the general information you will need to know about any specific product. You will have to look into other reports to find more specific information, but at least you will know what exactly is going on here and plan accordingly.

**Inventory Age:**

You may think the name may be self-explanatory; that this report will give let you know how old your stock is. However, it has much more information than just that. It is true that here you can find out the age of your stock, which is very important if you want to avoid paying the long-term storage fee, but you have much more at your disposal.

In this report, you can find out what your price is, what the lowest price is (if there are other sellers selling this product), how many units you have in stock, and you will even receive some recommendations on how to proceed with the units you have in the fulfillment center.

**Manage FBA Inventory:**

Here you will find another report with general information about the inventory you have with FBA. In order to use it you will have to download a report, but once that is done, you can open it with an Excel spreadsheet, and you can review the information.

You can see which units are being used with FBA and which ones are not. You can also see the number of units you have in the fulfillment center, the space they are taking up, the number of units that are on the way, etc. This is very similar to the information you can find in the FBA inventory, but in an Excel document. The differences between this report and the "Amazon Fulfilled Inventory" report are minimum, so mostly it would be a matter of which one you like the most.

**Archive:**

The "Archive" report is very similar to the previous one, except that it includes your archived units. When you list a product with FBA, you will never be able to delete it from your FBA Inventory. However, as long as you do not have any stock at all, you can archive the listing, which basically hides it. This report will include your archived listings along with the ones that have not been archived.

**Inbound Performance:**

When you ship units to a fulfillment center, you have an inbound performance, which basically means that they are tracking that what you indicated you would send and what you actually sent matches. Sending fewer or more units than indicated in your shipping plan can cause a delay at the fulfillment centers, so they want to make sure you do it right.

If you continually have problems with your shipments, this will affect your inbound performance, and if it continues to be affected, you may lose the ability to ship units to the fulfillment center. This is one of the reasons why it is very important to always request investigation for any discrepancy found in a shipment.

In this report, you will find information about your inbound performance so that you can see how the performance is, when there have been issues, and for which FNSKUs. Ideally, this should be empty, but if it is not, be careful to not let it fill up any more than what it is.

**Exportable Inventory:**

You will not find all that much information on this report. When we were setting up the FBA settings, there was an option for exportation. The choice you made there will determine what you see in this report. Basically, you will see a list of your products and whether they are eligible or not

**Excess Inventory:**

This report could be very useful for you. What it does is to calculate the number of units you have and how many sales, and it will determine whether it really is worth it to have those units in the fulfillment center. That way, you can remove any extra units you may have and plan any future shipments with fewer units so that you will not end up spending more than what you are making.

What you will see here is a list of your products with the SKUs, ASINs, and FNSKUs, the number of units you have, the number of sales, the estimated excess, etc. You will even see some recommendations of what to do, which in some cases will be to just remove your inventory and ship it back when you have sold most of what is already being stored.

**Bulk Fix Stranded Inventory:**

There may be times in which you could have stranded inventory. This means that you have units in the fulfillment center, but you do not have an active listing for them. This could occur for a number of reasons; for example, if you send units and they were found to be a similar product than what you had listed, but not the same one.

This is more than just a report; it is like a flat-file, or a feed, with which you can fix any stranded inventory you may have. You download the document, open it up in an Excel spreadsheet, add your price and condition, and then you upload it like you would any other feed. If you have an individual selling plan, this will not be possible.

**Subscribe & Save Performance:**

Now we have finished with the inventory reports, and we have reached the ones related to sales. The "Subscribe & Save Performance" report is similar to one we saw earlier about the same program, but that one was about forecasting. This one will tell you all about your current performance regarding this program.

**Amazon Fulfilled Shipments:**

This is a great place to see all of the sales you made in a specific month's time-frame, all in an Excel spreadsheet. You will be able to choose a specific number of days or set exact dates, and then you can request the download of the report that will show all of the shipments that Amazon has made for your products.

With this report, you can go back up to 18 months in the past, but the dates that you choose cannot be any more than 31 days. If you need any more than that, what you can do is to generate several reports and then copy and paste them all into one spreadsheet.

**All Orders:**

There are two options to see the "All Orders" reports: normal, and XML. Regardless of which one you choose, you will see the same information, which is a report of all the orders for FBA, whether they have been shipped or not.

This report is very similar to the previous one, except that, as mentioned in the previous paragraph, this one will also show the sales that have not been shipped yet. As with the previous report, you will not be able to request a report for more than 31 days.

**Customer Shipment Sales:**

This is very similar to the "Amazon Fulfilled Shipments" report, but there are some important differences. For one thing, you are not limited to only 31 days. Instead, you can have a range of up to a year and a half. The other difference is that this report is viewed online rather than being downloaded like the previously mentioned one.

**Promotions:**

If you are the kind of person who likes to be on top of everything and make sure that the system is working effectively, you might be looking at each of the orders to make sure that the customer paid what you are expecting them to pay. At times, you may see that there was some type of rebate applied to the order. If that is the case, you can come to this report to see why that happened.

In many cases, this could happen because of the "Super Saver Shipping" promotion, or the free trial of Prime that some customers use. You may be wondering how this will affect you, but rest assured that it will not. You will still receive the same payment as if no promotion had been applied; this report is only informative, and does not mean that you are losing any money.

**Monthly Storage Fees:**

Now we have reached the "Payments" section of the reports. The name of this report is pretty self-explanatory; it tells you how much you have paid for each month's storage fee. You will see a list of all the products, the dimensions, the weight, and how much you paid.

**Fee Preview:**

The "Fee Preview" report is another one with a very self-explanatory name, except that you will not only see the fee that you should pay, but also the reason why. You can already see the FBA fees to be paid in the inventories, but here you can see the dimensions, the weight, and the amount you will have to pay for each product.

In case you think you are paying higher fees than you should, check this report out. It could offer you some insight as to why you are paying this amount, and if there is any incorrect information, you can contact Seller Support to find out how to correct it.

**Long Term Storage Fee Charges:**

This report is very similar to the "Monthly Storage Fees" report, except that these fees are only charged twice a year. If you recall from an earlier section of this chapter, the amount you will pay depends not only on how much you have, but how long it has been in the fulfillment center. This report will show all of this information for each product for which this fee has been charged.

**Reimbursements:**

There will be times in which Amazon will give you some type of reimbursement, whether it be for damaged units, lost inventory, etc. Normally, when they issue a reimbursement for FBA, they will give you a reimbursement ID. If they do not, and you are the kind of person who likes to keep records of everything, reopen the case and request the ID.

This report will show you each of the reimbursements that you have received for FBA issues. It will show you the ID, the product, the date, and the reason why you received the reimbursement.

**FBA Customer Returns:**

Now we have reached the "Customer Concessions" section of the reports. When using FBA, it is important to take into account that Amazon will treat your stock the same way they would treat their own. This is in the agreement that you accepted when you started to use FBA, so you will not be able to complain about this.

There will be moments in which customers will purchase your products and then return them. In almost all the cases, Amazon will accept the returns. I know this could be annoying, but normally this is not a large percentage, so it should not affect your income.

Whenever there is a return, no matter what the reason was, it will show up in this report. You will see the order ID, the product, the generic reason (which is from a list of options they can choose when requesting the return), and the status of the product, which means whether it is sellable, customer damaged, or defective. You will see more about these statuses later on in another section of this chapter.

If you realize that a full refund was given to a customer due to a return, but you check this report and do not see the return reported here, it means that it has not arrived at the fulfillment center yet. Amazon will not wait for the unit to actually arrive to reimburse. You may be thinking that this could cause you to lose money, but do not worry; you will not lose anything. If after 45 days the unit has not returned, you will receive reimbursement automatically. If the return was due to an Amazon error, you will also receive reimbursement for it.

**Replacements:**

At times, instead of returning a unit, a replacement may needed. An example is the following: If a customer buys a product, Amazon ships it, but for some reason it never arrives, the customer will certainly call to find out what happened. Amazon may offer a refund, but a replacement may be offered instead, so that the customer can receive what was ordered.

Again, you should not lose money because of something like this. In many cases, your unit may return to the fulfillment center, so you will not have lost anything. If not, you should receive an automatic refund. If you do not, contact Seller Support and ask about it. They may show you where you can see that it did in fact return, or they may issue a manual reimbursement. Either way, Amazon will be responsible.

**Recommended Removal:**

We have reached the final section of the reports, which is "Removals." If you set up FBA to automatically remove unsellable or aged inventory, then you will have no need for this report. If you did not, then the "Recommended Removal" report will let you know which units are either damaged (in a way that Amazon is not responsible) or aged.

You should see a list of all units that are recommended to be removed. If you do not mind paying the long-term storage fee, then you do not have to worry about the aged inventory. However, any unsellable units will be automatically destroyed after 30 days if you do not remove it.

This report is not only informative; you will also have an option to remove all of the recommended inventory. If you do not want to remove everything, that is ok. You just select that option, and when you are taken to the next page, you will have the option to take any units off of the list so that they are not removed.

**Removal Order Detail:**

This report is helpful to find out about the removal orders that have been done. You will see here not only the removals that you requested, but also the ones that have been done by the system, like when you have automatic removals activated.

**Removal Shipment Detail:**

This is very similar to the previous report, but more detailed. You will be able to download a report in which you can see the removals, tracking numbers, disposition, and more. If you have several removals going on at the same time, this report is perfect to keep track of them.

## Reconciliations

As I mentioned previously, there is a report in which you can reconcile your inventory, but I always recommend doing it manually, since the report is not totally accurate. In this short section, I will teach you how to perform a manual reconciliation. Now for this you can only go back a year and a half, but that should be enough, since you will not be able to make a claim for any discrepancies that are before that time. Please keep in mind that this process is done individually for each product.

In order to reconcile your inventory, your first step is to set a starting date. If you have been selling since before that date, then you will need to go to the "Daily Inventory History" report to see how many units you had that day. Once you have that number, you can begin.

Now that you know how many units you are starting out with, you will have to go to five other reports. The first one is the "Received Inventory" report, which tells you how many units have been received at the fulfillment center so far. Add that number to the starting number.

Your next step is to find the "Customer Shipment Sales"

report. You will see how many units have been shipped by FBA to your customers, so you can subtract that number. So, for example, if you started out with seven units and found three more in "Received Inventory," then you would have ten. Then if you found six units sold, then you would have four left.

The "Returns" report is the next one to look for. It is important to know how many units that have been sold have come back. It does not matter whether they are sellable or not, though; it just matters that they returned. If you find any units here, you will have to add them.

Now you need to know how many units have been removed. Go to the "Removal Order Detail" report and look for all removals made for the product you are investigating. Once you have found them, click on the order ID, and you will see how many units were removed, and that number will be subtracted.

Finally, you will need to check inventory adjustments. Here, you are looking for misplaced and found units. You will see negative numbers for the misplaced and positive numbers for the found, so do the math and find out how many are actually misplaced. If all of them have been found, the result may be zero.

Now one thing that must be taken into consideration is that not all of the misplaced units are really misplaced. Remember that when there are virtual overages, they are reported here, so keep a record of your shipments and the number of overages that are virtual so that you can take that into account when calculating this.

The result you may find once you have finished calculating the inventory adjustments may be positive or negative. If it is positive, add that number to the full calculation of the reconciliation. If the number is negative, subtract it.

Once you have finished with the calculation, the number you have found should be the same number in your inventory. This will not necessarily be the number of sellable units. You will have to add sellable, unsellable, and reserved to see if the numbers match. If they do, then everything is working fine. If not, contact Seller Support.

**Lost and Damaged Inventory**

When you look at the "Inventory Adjustments" report, you may see some misplaced units once in a while. If this happens, do not panic; Amazon will reimburse the missing unit if it is not found. When a unit goes missing, Amazon will take 35 days to search for it. If it is found, you will see a "found" event in "Inventory Adjustments." If 35 days have gone by and it has not been found, Amazon will reimburse automatically.

While looking at your inventory, you may find sometimes that there are unfulfillable units. If this is the case, it is crucial that you see what the status is, because depending on the reason why it is unfulfillable, Amazon may or may not owe you money. To find out, you should click on the number under "Unfulfillable" in your inventory (this should be the normal inventory, and not the Amazon-Fulfilled one), and you will see more details about your damaged units.

**Defective or Customer Damaged:**

If you see that there are units that show as either "Defective" or "Customer Damaged," there is not much to do. As I mentioned before, you agreed that Amazon would treat your stock as their own, and they will almost always accept return requests.

If the customer contacts Customer Service and says that the product is defective, the return will be processed, and nobody is going to check your product to see if it really is defective or not. You will have to remove it and determine its state yourself.

If the customer returns it for any other reason, for example, because he or she just did not want it anymore, then Amazon will process the return (if it is still inside the time-frame in which customers are allowed to return). If it arrives at the fulfillment center damaged, then it will be placed as "Customer Damaged." Again, you will have to remove it and determine whether it can be sold again or not.

It is important to keep in mind that Amazon will not reimburse for either of these situations. It does not matter how much you threaten or escalate; the policy says that no reimbursement is due.

**Damaged in the Warehouse:**

If you see this message, it means that at some point, somebody at the fulfillment center probably dropped your product and damaged it. Do not remove these items; if you do, Amazon will not reimburse. They will automatically disappear from your inventory, and you will receive an automatic reimbursement after 30 days.

**Carrier Damaged:**

Just like with the previous type of damage, you should not

remove any units that show as "Carrier Damaged." This means that Amazon shipped the item to a customer, but it arrived damaged, so the customer rejected the delivery and it was returned to the fulfillment center.

If you notice any units with this kind of damage, contact Seller Support immediately. They will investigate the issue, and if it is determined that the item was in fact damaged by the carrier, then you will receive a reimbursement. This does not include any items damaged by the carrier you used to ship to Amazon, though.

**Distributor Damaged:**

This may cause some alarm if you see this, but do not panic; if you see this type of damage, it does not mean that you sent a damaged unit. The way you will proceed depends on which carrier you used when you shipped your products to the fulfillment center.

If you used any carrier that is not the Amazon-Partnered Carrier, then you will have to remove the item and submit a claim to your carrier, since Amazon is not responsible for any damages caused by the carrier that you used. If you used UPS or FedEx, but in your shipment plan you did not select to use an Amazon-Partnered Carrier, then it does not count as being a partnered carrier, since you are the client, and not Amazon.

If you shipped your items with the partnered carrier, then Amazon will be responsible. Contact Seller Support, and they will investigate to find out whether they were in fact damaged by the carrier or if you damaged them before shipping them. Normally, the investigation will show that it was the carrier's fault, and you will receive a reimbursement.

# Sponsored Products

If you are an active buyer in Amazon, or if you are the kind of seller that constantly searches for your own products to test their searchability, you may have noticed that there are sponsored products at the top of the search. You can have your products featured here as well.

The main aspect you need to know about this program is that it is pay-per-click. In other words, you do not pay just to have your products showing in the "Sponsored Products" section; you will only pay when somebody actually clicks on it.

You may be wondering how much each click costs. What is interesting is that the price depends on you. You will have the option to choose how much you want to pay each time somebody clicks on your product. This is called a "bid." You set the bid for how much you will pay for each click, and your product will be sponsored depending on the keywords you chose and your bid price. If somebody has a higher bid than yours, their product will have priority.

There is actually no way to find out how much the other bids are, so do not contact Seller Support to ask that; not even they have a way to know. Just set a price that you are comfortable with, and check out the results. If you notice that your products are not being viewed enough, then you can increase your bid.

You will also be able to set the amount of money you will spend each day. For example, if you want to only spend $5 a day, you can set it up that way. If each click costs $0.50, then you will be able to receive ten clicks per day. Once your product has been clicked on ten times, your $5 will have run out, and your product will no longer be sponsored until the next day.

**The Buy Box**

One aspect that you must take into account is that in order for this program to function properly, you should be winning the Buy Box. This means that when somebody views your product, it shows your name as the main seller, and you see a button that says "Add to Cart." If not, your Sponsored Products campaign might be benefitting another seller.

Sometimes, no seller will have the buy box on a specific product. If that happens, you will see a button that says "See All Buying Options" where the Buy Box should go. This can be seen in the following image:

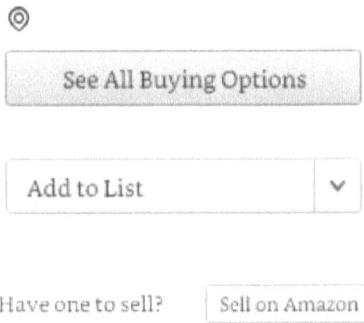

When a customer clicks on the "See All Buying Options" button, they will see a list of each of the sellers who have listed this product, the condition they sell it in, and their price. If there is a Buy Box, you will see an option to set quantity, it will show a price, the seller who is winning the Buy Box, and the options to either add the product to the cart, or to buy it immediately. This can be seen in the following image:

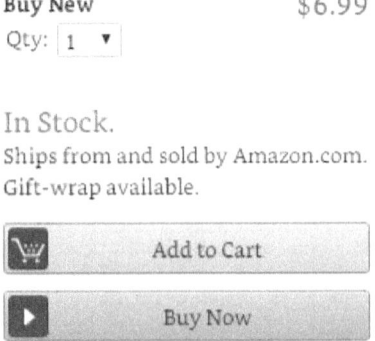

As you can see in the picture, Amazon is winning the Buy Box for that product. If your name is not there, then do not start a Sponsored Products campaign, as you will only be helping the seller who is winning it.

Winning the Buy Box is not easy, and there are many factors that influence this. Basically, you have to offer the best deal regarding price, availability, and how quickly your customer can receive it. Sometimes, you may be winning the Buy Box in one area, but in another area you are not. For example, if you live in Texas, then you might win the Buy Box for anybody in Texas who is shopping on Amazon. But somebody in Maine may see that another seller is winning the Buy Box, just because that seller is much closer to Maine and can deliver quicker.

## Creating a Campaign

In order to create a Sponsored Products campaign, hover the cursor over the "Advertising" tab and click "Campaign Manager," and then, "Create a Campaign." Next you will see a page in which you will add the information of the campaign you wish to create.

You should give your campaign a name, which is only for your visibility, just so you can distinguish one campaign from another. You will then select your daily budget, and a date range. You can leave the end date as "No end date" so that it will continue indefinitely.

Once you have set that information, it is time to select a targeting type. You can choose from automatic or manual targeting. If you choose automatic, Amazon will automatically show your products to all customers who search for any products like yours. Usually this is the best option, since most of the time it offers better results. If you choose the manual targeting, you will have to enter a series of keywords, and people will only see your products when they type in those specific words.

Click on the "Continue to next step" button, and you will be asked to name your ad group. If your campaign deals with different types of products, you can have several ad groups, and naming them helps you distinguish one from another.

After naming your ad group, you can set your bid, and then add your products. You can search them by name, SKU, or by ASIN. Search for your products and click the "Select" button. Once you have selected all of them, click the "Save and finish" button. Now you will have to wait around an hour for your campaign to be visible on Amazon.

## Bulk Operations

If you would like to make changes to existing campaigns or create new ones in bulk, there is an option to do so with a flat-file. In order to do so, you can go to your campaign manager and select the "Bulk operations" tab. Select a date range, and click on the "Create bulk file for download" button.

Once you have downloaded the file, open it up as a spreadsheet and add the necessary information. Some fields will need no entry, so just see what exactly needs to be filled in.

In this file, you can edit existing campaigns and/or add new ones. Once you have added all the information needed, save the file, and return to the "Bulk operations" section of the Campaign Manager. You will see another tab that says "Upload." Click on that, and you will be able to upload your file.

Wait for the upload to be processed, and once it is done, you can see the status. If there are any errors, you can download a processing report that will tell you what the errors are, so that way you can correct them.

## Bid+

If you would like for your campaigns to have more of a chance to show up, you may want to consider using Bid+. With this feature, your bid can increase to up to 50%, but only when needed. It will only increase just enough for your ad to show up.

An example is the following: If you have a bid of $1 per click, Bid+ can increase it to $1.50. If someone else has a bid of $1.25, Bid+ will make your bid increase to $1.26 so that your product will show up instead of the other seller's product. The only drawback is that in order to use this feature, you have to use manual targeting.

In order to enable Bid+, search for your campaign and click on it. Click on the "Campaign" tab, and at the bottom, you will see an option to enable Bid+. Click on that option, and this feature will be enabled for the campaign that you selected.

## Campaign Performance

Now that your campaign is complete, you can review the performance at any time. By going back to the Campaign Manager, you can see the status of your campaign, the daily budget, impressions (which means the number of times your ad was shown in the search results), clicks, the amount of money you have spent, sales, and the cost of sales, which is a percentage of what you have spent on the campaign. Some of this information is only visible once you have clicked on the campaign.

It is important to take a look at the performance regularly to see how you are doing. If you see that there are many clicks, but people are not buying your product, you can review the product and/or the campaign to see if something can be improved.

## Reports

The performance you see in the campaign manager is not the only source of information you have access to. You can also download reports of your campaigns in case you want to keep a separate record.

Hover the cursor over the "Reports" tab and select the "Advertising Reports" option. You will see "Performance Over Time," "Performance by SKU," "Performance by Placement," "Search Term Report," "Other ASIN Report," and "Campaign Performance Report."

Choose which type of report you want, and then select the date range you want the report to show, and click on the "Request Report" button. Ahead, you will see a brief description of each of the reports that you can view here.

**Performance Over Time:**

Here, you will be able to see how many clicks there have been, the average cost-per-click, and the total you have spent. You can view the report online without downloading it, but then on the top-right corner of the report, you will find an option to download it.

**Performance by SKU:**

This will show information about each individual product. You will be able to see the information about how many times your ad has been displayed and how many clicks there have been for each product that you have campaigns for.

**Performance by Placement:**

This report is only useful if you are using Bid+. If you do not use this feature, then you can ignore the "Performance by Placement" report. If you are using Bid+, then here you will be able to compare the performance of your campaign before and after enabling this feature, so you can decide whether it really is working for you or not.

**Search Term Report:**

This report is especially useful if you are using manual targeting. What this will show you is what the customers wrote to trigger your ad to be shown in their search results. If a certain keyword is not showing up here, you might want to consider replacing it for one that could be more useful.

**Other ASIN Report:**

When a customer clicks on one of your ads, they may purchase that product, although in some cases, they may end up buying another one of your ASINs that was not being promoted. This report will show you each of the ASINs that were bought under these circumstances.

**Campaign Performance Report:**

This report is similar to the one you see in the Campaign Manager. You will find information about sales for each campaign, SKU and keyword information, and other relevant information that will help you determine whether your campaign is working properly or not.

By using a combination of each of these reports, you will have a better understanding of how your campaigns are working, and with this knowledge, you can make any necessary changes. In some cases, you may have to experiment with different tactics before you find the best way to manage your campaigns, and these reports will help you to do just that.

# Ungating and Brand Registry

Although ungating and Brand Registry are two different topics, I decided to add them both together into the same chapter due to the fact that they have many similarities, and they are both applications that follow similar processes. Ungating is the process of obtaining approval for restricted products, while Brand Registry is the process of (as the name states) registering your brand in Amazon to have more control over your listings.

## Ungating

There are several reasons why products can be restricted; sometimes it is because they can be a safety hazard, so it is important to make sure that what you are selling is authentic and not a dangerous copy. Another reason can be because it is such a popular brand that it is frequently copied, so in this way, you can prove that what you are selling is the real thing.

If you want to sell a restricted product, be prepared to submit documentation. In some cases, the process is simple, and you will only have to send invoices that prove that you bought the products from a distributor. In other cases, you will have to submit more technical documentation.

Now the question that some may be asking is, "How can you tell whether a product is restricted or not?" That is very simple; just try to add the product to your inventory, and if it is restricted, you will see something that says "Listing limitations apply." If you click on that, it will tell you exactly which type of limitations, and you will see a button that says "Request approval," as seen below:

1 to 1 of 1 Results

A Christmas Story Kurt Adler UL 10-Lights Leg Lamp Light Set
UPC: 086131274855
EAN: 0086131274855
Sales Rank:370833
11 New & Used Offers
See all product details

⚠ Listing limitations apply

- You need approval to list Lighting products

Request approval

Click on the "Request approval" button, and you will begin the ungating process. You will be taken to another page in which you will see the category or brand for which you need approval, and then you will have to click another button that says "Request approval."

The next page you will see will have a form for you to fill out. The first question is extremely important, and you must respond with utmost honesty, since this could change the way the process will work for you. You will be asked if you are a reseller/distributor, manufacturer, or both. If you manufacture your own products, the requirements will be different from what a reseller or distributor would have to submit. If you are requesting approval for a brand, you will not see this question.

If you chose the option of being a reseller/distributor, you will have to submit at least one invoice. It should contain at least ten units of the product you are trying to add to your account, your full name and address, the name and address of the manufacturer or distributor, and it should not be more than 180 days old. Also, although the help page does not say this on the application page, the distributor's address should be searchable on Google. If they cannot find a website with this address, the invoice will not be valid, and you will not receive approval.

After uploading the invoice, you will have the option to add some comments. Most of the time, this will not be of any help, unless there are details of the invoice that you need to clarify. You can then add an e-mail address and a phone number, although adding a number will do you no good at all; they will most likely never call you.

If you are a manufacturer, you most likely will not have to provide any type of invoice. There are some cases in which you will have to, but the invoice should show the purchase of the raw materials you use to create the product you are selling.

Apart from the invoice, you may have to provide some additional documentation, like a Declaration of Conformity, a Quality Management Systems Certification, pictures of the box (which should have the logo on it), among others. These are just some examples, and it does not necessarily mean that you will have to provide all at once.

Of all the documents requested, one of the most commonly rejected ones is the Declaration of Conformity. If your product does not comply with the safety standards, this document will reflect that, and you will not receive approval for this type of product.

You may be thinking that you are about to find out exactly what you have to add to this document in order to pass the ungating process; if that is the case, then you would be wrong. This book is not intended to help you cheat the system, and if you have a product that does not comply with safety standards, then it is dangerous, and you should not be selling it.

If your documents comply with the requirements, then you will be approved, and the restriction will be lifted. It will usually take some time for the system to be updated; in the e-mail you will receive granting the approval, you will be told that it takes 24 hours, but it usually takes less.

If the documents do not comply, then they will let you know exactly which ones are lacking. If the invoices are insufficient, you will be told exactly why. For some other documents, you will be told as well; however, you will never be told why the Declaration of Conformity does not comply. The reason behind this is that if they tell you, then you could edit the document and add false information to receive the approval.

As I mentioned before, you will most likely not receive any phone calls from the agents who work on your application. Imagine your receive a phone call from an agent saying that your documents do not comply; you would obviously want to know why, and if you ask and the agent refuses to answer, you might get angry. If they do not call you, this situation can be avoided, so they will respond by e-mail.

If you are requesting approval for a brand, then you will only have to upload one document. This could either be an invoices showing that you have purchased this product, or a letter from the brand owner authorizing you to sell. If you choose to send an invoice, it will have the same requirements mentioned.

Once you submit any ungatng request, you will see a screen in which you will be thanked for your application. Under that, you will see a link that says "Check status of your request." Click on that, and you will see a screen that looks like this:

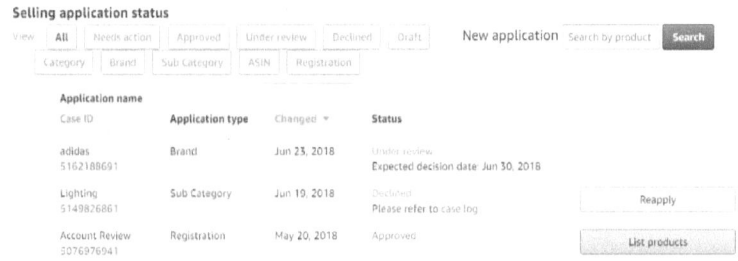

In my personal account, there are three applications showing there. One is for Adidas, another for lighting, and another for registration. The registration just will always be approved if you have submitted the identification and bank documents that were mentioned in the first chapter. Lighting shows as declined because it was only a test application that was made. The Adidas application shows as under review for now.

As you can see for the lighting application, since it was declined, there is the option to reapply. No matter how many times an ungating request has been rejected, you will always be able to apply again and again. Once you have received approval, you will see a button that says "List products."

## GTIN Exemption

Although GTIN exemption is technically not ungating, I am including it in the same category since the logic behind it is very similar. With this process, you are requesting a certain type of approval, and without it you will not be able to list certain products, so it is very similar.

As you already know, in order to add products on Amazon, they need to have barcodes. However, what if you have a product that does not have one? What if you make your own products and do not want to spend the money buying barcodes for them? Does that mean you will never be able to sell them on Amazon? The good news is that you can, as long as you have GTIN exemption.

A GTIN is an identifier. It can mean a UPC, an EAN, an ISBN, etc., which are all related to the identifiers that go on the barcodes. If your products do not have anything like that, just look for a help page in Seller Central called "How to list products that do not have a GTIN (UPC, EAN, JAN, or ISBN)."

In this help page, you will find all the information you need about this process, and at the bottom you will see the option to request the approval. There are several different paths to take when applying, which are all covered in this help page, but you will also see them in this section of this book.

Sometimes, you may find brands for which none of the products have identifiers. If that is the case, you will need to provide either a letter from the brand owner stating that the products do not have identifiers, a list of sample products, or a link to a website in which the products can be viewed.

If by any chance you are unable to contact the brand owner and there is no website, you still have an option. You can upload pictures to an online image service and then send the link in your application. That way you can prove that they do not have the identifiers normally needed to list them.

If you are able to the brand owner to request a letter, be sure that said letter meets all the requirements. The letter should include the brand owners name and contact information, plus your own contact information, which should include your address, phone number, and either your e-mail address, or a website address. Of course, it should be legible, and it should be in English (or in the language of the marketplace you are applying in). Finally, the letter should state that their products do not have a GTIN.

In the GTIN exemption help page, you will find a template letter that you can send to the brand owner so that they can write it out easily. This could help so that you can get it right the first time and not have to apply a second time.

If you are unable to provide a letter nor a website, then you can send a list. In the same help page, you will find several Excel templates depending on the situation. Look at each of the templates and choose which one is best. Fill it out, and then request approval.

One important aspect that must be taken into account is that if your exemption is based on a brand, whenever you add products, you must write the brand name exactly how it was approved; it is case-sensitive, so be careful how you make the request.

If the exemption is not for a specific brand, you will have to provide SKUs. Again, you will have to add your products with that exact SKU, being case-sensitive as well.

Another crucial aspect is the key attribute. GTIN exemptions are usually approved with some type of attribute, which is usually either model number or part number. Whichever it may be, you must add that in order for the exemption to work. You will find both in "More Details" when adding a new product. If you cannot see this tab, then activate the "Advanced View." You can add any number you want. Most sellers just add the same SKU here.

If you are the manufacturer of the products, you can send a letter that you can write yourself stating that you are the brand owner and that you do not use GTINs, or just submit either the list or the website. However, if this is the case, the best course of action, instead of requesting an exemption, is to apply for Brand Registry. It is more complicated, but it has more benefits.

## Brand Registry

In some ways, Brand Registry is very similar to GTIN exemption, except that it is designed specifically for your own brand. That is not all, though; if you already have a GTIN on your products, you can still use this feature to make sure that nobody else can make changes on your listings, and you have access to many more features like Enhanced Brand Content, Headline Search Ads, and Storefronts, all that can help you sell more!

Unlike most aspects of Amazon's seller platform, the Brand Registry application is not done through Seller Central. In order to apply, you must go to brandregistry.amazon.com. If you are already signed into your seller account, you will see a sign-up form with some of your information already there.

In this form, you will have to enter your business title and company name, and then you will have to select if your business is incorporated or not. If you have a corporation, select that it is incorporated. If not, then just say no. You will then have to choose between a call and a text message to verify your phone number. Once you have done that, you will have to verify with a captcha and click on the "I have read and accepted the Amazon Brand Registry terms and conditions" checkbox, and click save.

Congratulations; you now have a Brand Registry account. This is important, because any inquiries you may have about your brand should be asked here instead of on Seller Central. This platform has its own "Contact Us" feature which is accessed in a very similar way as in Seller Central, and there is a team specialized in helping brand owners with their Brand Registry.

In the Brand Registry home page, you will see an option that says "Enroll a new brand." Click on that in order to begin. You will then be asked if your products and packaging have a permanently affixed brand name and logo. If they do not, stop what you are doing and make sure that your products do get one, since if you say no, this could affect the outcome.

The next question is if you intend to enroll more than ten brands. The answer to this question is not relevant in terms of whether or not you will receive approval; just click either yes or no, then enter your brand name and click "Next." If you do intend to sell more than 10, a Brand Support agent will contact you to assist you with the process.

The next step is to provide the trademark. This could either be text or design mark, but if you choose the design mark, it should still say the name of your brand. There are logos that include the name, and others that do not. For example, the Nike logo is similar to a checkmark. It does not say the brand name, but if you see it, you immediately know what type of product it is. That type of logo does not work in this case, though, since it should say your brand's name as well.

You will then have to choose the trademark number and the office in which it is registered. This is extremely important; if your brand is not registered in a trademark office, you will never receive approval for your brand. Moreover, you must choose the correct office and trademark number; the agent who will look over your application will go to that trademark office's website to search for your brand, and if it is not there, your application will be denied.

For the European marketplaces, this can be tricky, since there are offices for several European countries, and then a general one for the European Union. If you registered in the Spanish office but chose the European Union one in the application, your application will be denied since the agent will not find the brand anywhere.

Click next, and then you will reach the final page. Here, you will have to select whether your products have GTINs or not. If they do not, you will receive a key attribute just like in GTIN exemption. If they do, then you will not receive a key attribute, but everything else will work the same.

You will then be asked if you sell your products online. If you do not, this is not a problem. However, having a personal website helps verify the brand.

In the next question, you will be asked if your brand has an existing Seller or Vendor relationship. Since your seller account is most likely for selling this brand, then you will choose "Seller." If you have a vendor account as well, then you can choose "Both." You will be asked for the e-mail address associated to the account(s), so enter it there.

Then you will be asked if your brand manufactures products, if it licenses trademarks to others who manufacture the products, and then the locations where they are manufactured and distributed. Depending on your answers, more questions may show up, so just answer honestly, as this will not have effect on the outcome. Once you have answered these questions, just click the "Submit application" button to finish.

You will receive a "Thank you" message, and there you can either click "Done" or start another application right there. If you go back to the Brand Registry home page, you will now see that you have a brand under review. Just wait for the application to be reviewed and responded to, and you will find out whether you are approved or not.

You may be asked for additional information, so just answer everything and send whatever is requested, and you should not have any problems. Once you have received approval, you will have access to the features that will be described in the remainder of this chapter.

## Enhanced Brand Content

Once you have received approval for your brand, you will have access to something called "Enhanced Brand Content." If you look at the Amazon detail pages, you will see that most products look normal, but others look very different. If you look for products made by big brands, you will see that the detail page has more content and looks better.

In the case of the big brands, this is called "A+ Content," and it is for vendors. However, Enhanced Brand Content (EBC) is very similar. You must have a professional seller plan for this, so you will have to make sure you are willing to pay the monthly subscription fee in order to use this feature. For many people, it is worth it, since you will be able to add pictures to your description, and you can even add videos to your products.

In order to create EBC, you will have to hover the cursor over the "Advertising" tab in Seller Central and click "Enhanced Brand Content." If you do not have a brand approved, you will not see this option, since it is exclusive to brand owners.

You will reach the EBC page, and there you will enter the SKU that you would like to edit, and click the "Get Started" button. After that, you will be able to choose from the various templates that are available, and add all the relevant information and content.

Once you have submitted the content, it will be reviewed. This can take up to seven days, but usually it is done faster than that. If it is not approved, you will be able to see the exact reasons why, so just make the necessary edits, and submit it again.

Some common errors are adding your specific information to the content or any warrantees or guarantees. Even though this is your brand, other sellers could be able to purchase your products and sell them as well, so because of this, the information must be about the product itself. Another mistake is adding blurry pictures to the content. For more information about what is restricted, you can look for a help page called "Create Enhanced Brand Content" in which you will see all of the restrictions.

Once your content is approved, you will be able to see it on your detail page. Now it will look much more professional, and your potential customers will probably find the page to be much more appealing, increasing their chances of buying your product.

## Headline Search Ads

Headline Search Ads is very similar to Sponsored Products,

except that instead of just promoting specific products, you are promoting your brand in general. You can choose a logo, a custom message, and set it up so that when the customers click on it, they will be redirected to your storefront, which is the place where they can see all of your products.

In order to create a campaign, hover the cursor over the "Advertising" tab and click "Campaign Manager," which will only be available if you have a brand approved. Keep in mind that you must have a professional selling plan in order to create your campaign. If not, change your selling plan before you continue.

On this page, you will see any existing campaigns. You will also see a button that says "Create Campaign." Click on that button in order to begin. Select the brand you want to create a campaign for; if you have more than one, then you will have to create separate campaigns for each of them.

Your next step will be to choose whether you want your customers to be directed to your storefront, or a product list page. Later on in this chapter you will learn more about the storefront, but if you would like to redirect them to a product list page, click on that option, and then add all of the ASINs you want to the list. You must choose at least three.

Click on the "Continue" button, and you will be able to modify the way your brand name will show up (which will be reviewed for approval) and add a headline. Then upload a brand image or select an image from one of your products. You will see a preview of the ad, so if you are satisfied, click "Continue."

Just like with Sponsored Products, you will now be able to set a bid. Once you have set that, you can set your keywords. This also works the same as with Sponsored Products, so I will not go into detail about that. Once you have finished that, set a campaign name, the duration, and the daily budget. You can then review your ad and click on the "Finish" button. It will then go through a review process, and you will be notified of the resolution.

## Storefront

Creating a Storefront is simple. Hover the cursor over the "Storefront" tab in Seller Central and click "Manage Stores." Just like the previous features mentioned here, you will need a brand approved in order to have access to the Storefront.

You will see a big orange button that says "Create Store." Click on that button, and you will be asked for which brand you want to create your store. You can create one for each brand that you have registered on Amazon. Next, you will be able to upload a brand logo, enter a brand description, and then you can choose from several templates. Ahead you will see a brief description of each of the templates.

**Marquee:**

With this template, you will be able to add a compilation of text, pictures, and videos that best describe your brand. If your brand deals with several different types of categories, you might want to choose this one.

**Highlight:**

On this template, you can show your top selling items. The pictures that you upload here will show up big on your store. If you do not have many products, you can add pictures of each of them on this template.

**Product Grid:**

With the Product Grid, you will be able to show many products at once. Usually this one is used if you have at least eight items, although it is most useful if your products are in the same category, or if they are similar categories.

Once you have chosen the template, add the products and the content that you want it to have, and then preview it. Once you are satisfied with it, submit your store and wait for approval.

# Performance

By allowing you to sell on Amazon, this company is taking a chance with you. It is said that Amazon's goal is to become the most customer-centric company of the world, so the same is expected from you. It is important to provide the best customer service possible. If you are using FBA, there are many aspects that you will not have to worry about, but regardless of who fulfills your orders, you will have to take care of your performance.

If you look at the tabs in Seller Central, you will see that the last one says "Performance." Here you will see everything related to your performance metrics as a seller. If they get too high (or low, depending on the metric, you run the risk of having your account suspended. If that happens, you can still have it reinstated, but it is best to avoid this altogether. In this chapter you will learn about each of the metrics you need to take care of, and how to get your account reinstated if Performance ever does suspend it.

## Performance Metrics

There are several metrics you will have to keep an eye on in your account. Each of them has a certain target, and as long as the target is not exceeded, you will be fine. Ahead, you will see each of the metrics and find out how they are affected so that you can avoid having negative numbers in your account.

**Order Defect Rate:**

Order Defect Rate (ODR), as the name states, deals with the percentage of orders with defects. You should keep this metric under 1%. In order to do that, offer the best customer experience possible and avoid negative feedback, A-to-Z Guarantee claims, and chargeback claims. You will see more information about each of these issues later on in this chapter.

**Product Policy Compliance:**

Unlike with ODR, there is no leniency here; the target is zero complaints. You will have to watch out for four different types compliance issues. The first is "Intellectual Property Complaint." Basically, do not steal somebody else's idea. For example, if you sell someone else's product with your own brand name, you are stealing that person's intellectual property.

Second is the "Product Authenticity Customer Complaints." If you say that your product is made out of a certain material, make sure it really is. Or if you say that your product is of a certain brand, do not sell a copy. Make sure that all of your products are authentic to avoid any complaints.

Then, you have to watch out for the "Product Safety Customer Complaints." As was mentioned before in the

"Ungating" section of this book; if your product is a safety hazard, you should not be selling it. Make sure that all of your products comply with the safety regulations, and nobody should complain.

**Listing Policy Violations:**

Finally, you will have to avoid breaking any policies with your listings. For example, do not list something as new if it is used. As long as you are not breaking policies, you should not have any problems with this metric.

**Late Shipment Rate:**

The target for this metric is under 4%, and as the name states, it deals with shipments that were shipped late. There are two aspects that need to be taken into account for Late Shipment Rate (LSR), which are the actual shipping date, and the confirmation date. Both dates should be the same.

With every order you receive, you will always see the expected ship date. On that date or before, you must have shipped and confirmed the order. If you shipped it on time but did not confirm it, this metric will be affected. If you confirmed it on time but did not ship it, it will also be affected. If you are using FBA, you will not have to worry about this metric.

**Cancelation Rate:**

This is also known as Pre-fulfillment Cancel Rate, and it refers to the number of times in which you cancel an order instead of actually fulfill it. Again, if you are using FBA, this metric is irrelevant to you. If you fulfill your orders, try not to ever cancel. If you run out of stock, be sure to update your inventory to reflect that. The only way in which you will not be penalized for cancelling is if the customer requests the cancellation. If for some reason you made a mistake and cannot fulfill the order, try to contact the customer, explain the situation, and request that they cancel.

**Valid Tracking Rate:**

When you confirm an order, it is important to add a valid tracking number. If you do not, this metric will go down. Your goal for this metric is 95%. This is another metric that you do not have to worry about if you use FBA. If you do not, then be sure that you always add tracking, and when you do, it must be valid.

**Late Responses:**

If a customer contacts you to ask a question, you are expected to answer in less than 24 hours. If you do not, it will affect this metric. Your goal for this metric is less than 10%, so try to answer all of your customers. Even if you use FBA, answer the customers, even if it is just to tell them to contact Amazon.

That is all for the metrics that can actually impact your account. There is also the Return Dissatisfaction Rate and the Customer Service Dissatisfaction Rate, but they are in Beta stage, and for now, they will not affect your account.

## Feedback and Customer Reviews

Although Customer Reviews will not affect your performance, I am including it here because it is very similar to feedback, and many sellers confuse the two of them. Feedback is the way customers evaluate you for the order, and a customer review is the way customers evaluate the product.

If customers are giving a lot of negative feedback, then it

would be a good idea to evaluate your selling practices to see if there is something that you can improve. If you do not, and you continue to receive negative feedback, your account could be suspended due to Order Defect Rate.

The good news is that not all feedback is permanent. If a customer breaks policy with the feedback, you can contact Seller Support and request for the feedback to be removed. For example, if the customer is evaluating the product instead of the order service, it will be removed. If profanities are used, or if there are threats or your personal information, it will be removed. If you are using FBA and negative feedback is given due to something that was Amazon's fault, it will also be removed.

The same goes for customer reviews. If you notice that a customer review is evaluating your order or uses profanities or any other aspect that breaks policy, contact Seller Support. These reviews can be removed as well.

## A-to-Z Guarantee Claims

The A-to-Z Guarantee claims are designed to ensure that customers receive the same quality customer service that Amazon gives when dealing with third party sellers. Unfortunately, even if you win the claim, it will still count for the Order Defect Rate, but at least Seller Performance will know that you won the claim, and that could influence their decision as to whether your account should be suspended or not.

Once you have received a claim, it will work almost like a trial. You will have the chance to defend yourself, and at the end there will be a verdict. You will have three days to respond, and this includes weekends. Go to the "Performance" tab and click "A-to-Z Guarantee Claims" in order to find your claim and respond.

Once you have represented your side, usually the guarantee team will contact you and the buyer to request additional information. Once the verdict has been delivered, if you do not agree, you will have the chance to appeal.

In order to avoid these types of claims, try to maintain a clear communication with the buyer. Be as polite as possible, and if you know that there will be a delay, offer a refund immediately. There will still be claims, because there will always be annoying customers that you just cannot satisfy, but that is why there is leniency with the Order Defect Rate. As long as you have many healthy orders, one claim should not affect you.

## Chargebacks

In many cases, chargebacks are not your fault. If you receive a chargeback claim, respond to it within seven days (including weekends) to represent your side. This will work just like an A-to-Z Guarantee claim. You and the buyer may be contacted, and then a decision will be made which you will be able to appeal.

In some cases, you may be held responsible for the claim, and Amazon will charge you. In other cases, the claim will be denied altogether, and the customer will not receive any refund at all. There are also cases in which Amazon will confirm that you are not responsible, but the customer is not either, so Amazon itself will issue a refund without charging you.

## Performance Notifications

Be sure to always keep an eye on your Performance notifications. Whenever there are issues with your account or with a listing, the answer is most likely there. If you have a metric that is turning red, they will inform you, and if any action needs to be taken to avoid losing your account, that is where the message will be, so do not ignore these notifications.

Usually, when there is some type of problem in your account, you will not only see the reason in these notifications, but you will also see the way in which you can solve them. If you have any Performance notifications, you will see a number in the little flag that is next to the "Amazon Seller Central" logo on the top-left corner of your account. If there is a number there, click on it.

## Reinstating a Suspended Account

Hopefully you will never have to deal with this, but if your account is ever suspended, you can have it reinstated. If this ever happens, you will receive a Performance notification indicating exactly which metric caused the suspension, and it will also notify you that you need to submit a Plan of Action (POA) in order to reinstate your account.

Your Plan of Action must be as detailed as possible, and you must accept full responsibility of what happened. If you send a plan that blames someone else for your metrics, you will never be reinstated, so even if it is not your fault, be creative and make it seem as though it was.

Your plan must have three major sections to it. First, you

must state the reason why your account was suspended. Mention the metric that was affected and any other information that may be necessary. If there are orders involved, mention the orders. If there are ASINs involved, mention the ASINs.

The more information you add to this section, the better, because Seller Performance will see that you do understand what is going on, and that way you can prove that you can solve the problem. If there are not many details, it may be more difficult.

Next, explain exactly why those orders or those ASINs were affected. If you used a carrier that did not perform well, explain the whole situation. If you did not perform as well because you did not have enough staff, mention that as well. If there are several reasons why this metric was affected, I recommend using bullet points for each one of them, which will make the next part much easier.

Now it is time to create your plan and explain how you are going to avoid this situation in the future. If you took my advice and used bullet points for the previous section, in this section you can use bullet points to solve each of the previous issues.

Provide a detailed explanation about how you are going to avoid these problems. It is extremely important that you do not mention refunds or any kind of action if things go wrong. If you do, you are not showing that you want to avoid the problem, but instead that you have a plan B if you have the same problems again.

Once you have finished creating your plan, go to the Performance notification that mentioned the issue, and you should see an option to send your Plan of Action. Send it there and wait for a response. If your plan is acceptable, your account will be reinstated. You might have some restrictions, like a temporary hold on your payments, or you might not be able to fulfill your own orders for a while, but at least you will be able to sell.

If the plan was not sufficient, you will receive a notification saying that your account was not reinstated, so you will have to review your plan to see what you did wrong. If you are in doubt, contact Seller Support so that they can help you out more.

# Contacting Seller Support

Although you have learned a lot from this book, and hopefully you will not have to contact too often to ask the basic questions, there will be times in which you will need to contact Seller Support. The platform works very well, but sometimes there will be glitches that you will need to solve. In other cases, you will have technical issues that are not glitches, but you will need a resolution nonetheless.

This chapter is intended to explain how you can contact Seller Support in a more effective way. If you know the best path to make this contact, you increase your chances of having a quicker response, which will ultimately help you get back in business.

To contact Seller Support, click on the "Help" option on the top-right corner. At the bottom, you will see the "Get Support" options. It will show the Amazon logo inside of a message box. Click on that, and you will see several options. Click on the one that seems the closest to what you want to inquire about. It may offer some information before you actually have to contact. If there is no useful information, then you will see the "Contact us" option at the bottom.

If none of the options have to do with your inquiry, just click the "Can't find what you need?" option. There, you will see the "Contact us" option at the bottom as well. Click on that, and you will be asked how Seller Support can help you. Type in your inquiry, and click "Get help." If you still do not find what you need, close the help window.

You will now be provided with some options regarding the issue you are contacting for. Be very careful which option you choose. Take into account that if you want to change the title of a product, the fact that you use FBA does not make this an FBA issue. In this case, you would click "Products and inventory."

Choose the option that best suits what you need to request, and then, depending on several factors, you might see three options. You could contact by e-mail, by chat, or by phone. There will be cases in which you will only be able to contact by e-mail, though. Choose the option you prefer, and submit your request.

When contacting, be sure to specify everything as detailed as possible. Think to yourself whether your message makes sense or not, or if they will have to request any additional information. Just like you have your seller metrics, Seller Support does as well, and if they have to contact you back to request information, you are affecting their metrics. It is always best if they can resolve the issue at once without having to ask anything else.

As a rule of thumb, if there is any documentation that you can provide, do not wait for them to request it. Just send it over so that you can receive a quicker response. Maybe it will not be needed, but what if it is? If you send it, no harm will come out of it, but if you do not and it was needed, then you will have to wait longer.

Another important aspect is to never send a long list. For example, if you have 250 ASINs that all need to be fixed, do not send a list of all of them in one case. If you do that, you are negatively impacting the agent who will work on the case (their metrics will be strongly affected), and it will take much longer for you to receive your resolution. It is better to break the list up in five per case, or in the most extreme cases, ten per case.

The most important aspect I want to mention is the survey at the end of the e-mail. When an agent resolves a case, you will be sent an e-mail with a survey at the end asking if you were satisfied with the support provided.

When you receive this survey, take into account that you are not evaluating the process nor Amazon. You are directly evaluating the agent who resolved the case. If that agent treated you well, give him a yes.

Sometimes agents may give you a response that you do not like. Maybe you wanted a refund, and you were told that it is not possible. This is not the agent's fault, so it is not fair to give a no for something that is policy. If that person was nice to you, give that person a yes, and then you will see a second survey in which you can evaluate Amazon directly.

There may be times in which you may think that the agent just dos not want to give you what you want, even though you think that it can be done. If you are in doubt, either reopen the case, or call back and escalate. You must understand that these agents do not want to deny you anything you have a right to, just because they do not want you to give them a no. If they can do what you want, trust me, they will do it.

Now just because one agent did something for you, it does not mean it is something that should be done. For example, if you received a defective return with FBA and you request a refund, Amazon does not have the obligation to give you the refund. If an agent actually grants it, the agent broke policy, so you should not expect all of them to do so. It would be unfair if you give an agent a no because another agent did something that was not allowed.

If a case was worked on by several agents, remember that this survey only evaluates the one who resolved the case. If a previous agent did not treat you well, just call and escalate. Give the case number and the name of the agent who did not treat you well, and they will deal with that person.

# Conclusion

As you have seen in this book, Selling on Amazon can be a great opportunity for you, but it is important to know how to do it. Whether you use FBA or not, there are still many areas of the seller platform that you need to keep an eye on, and it is crucial that you provide the best customer experience possible.

I truly hope that you have learned valuable information from this book. Of course, there are aspects of selling that can only be learned by experience, but if you read all of the information that I have provided to you, you should be on the right track.

I wish you the best of luck with your sales now. Selling on Amazon can be a little complicated at first, even with all of this information, but now that you have learned so much, with practice, it will become like second nature. You are now on your own. Not totally alone, though, because when in doubt, you can always contact Seller Support!

www.ingramcontent.com/pod-product-compliance
Lightning Source LLC
Chambersburg PA
CBHW020439220526
45464CB00002B/772